UMBERTO FRANZOI

THE DOGE'S PALACE IN VENICE

WITH 131 COLOUR PLATES

Library of Congress Catalog Card Number 72-189767
© Copyright 1973-1991 by Edizioni Storti - Venezia
All Rights reserved. Printed in Italy

INDEX

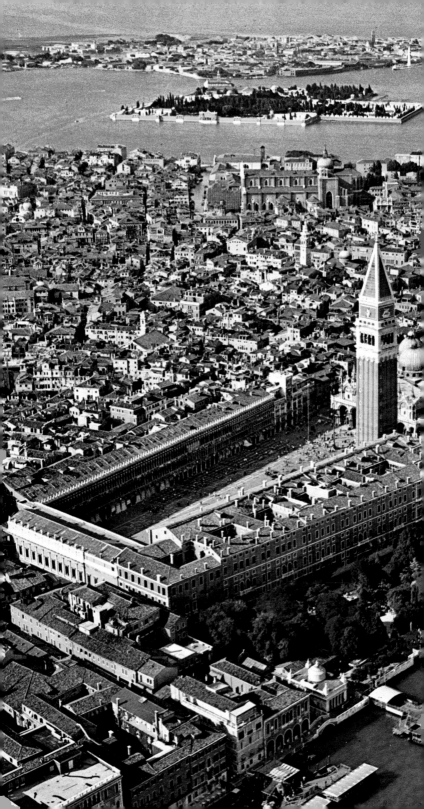

In 810, when Angelo Partecipazio transferred the government from Malamocco to the Rivoalto islands, he launched that long cycle of vivid, joyous and tragic events which make up the history of Venice. He wanted to set aside at once a definite area for the seat of this new power; then buildings would be erected. The first choice of a site, on a piece of land facing a large basin where several important waterways, communicating with the interior and with the sea, met, proved to be perfectly right. From that time on, in fact, there was never any question about its location. In the centuries which followed, this area developed. Here arose that monumental urban centre which was quickly established as the heart of the city, its political, religious and social core: St. Mark's Square. There the **Doges' Palace** was built as Venice grew during the second decade of the IX century. It was the seat of authority around which would alternately revolve individual interests sought and found in ever more distant lands.

With this idea in mind, the Most Serene Republic always gave special attention to the continuing expansion of the Doges' Palace. Over several centuries, enormous sums of money were lavished on the interior and exterior of the building, to make it the visible and explicit expression of an ideal concept: that of the political state. Today we can imagine what the original building looked like, reconstructing it in our minds from the few pieces of available information taken from documents of later periods which, in turn, come from much older chronicles. Remnants of foundations and walls suggest other aspects of its appearance. It must have been a building destined for defense, like a medieval castle with its nearly square plan. To be exact, it was enclosed by high walls with massive corner towers toward the basin side, and had fortified entrances. Within this enclosed area there were various buildings, probably against the walls themselves, where sat the governing bodies. The random placing of the offices inside the walls and the external continuity of the walls themselves influenced even in later periods the internal divisions of the uniform architectural complex. The subdivision of these governing and administrative branches must be discussed in the light of later developments, based on a systematic arrangement still in use when the Doges' Palace came in point of fact to have a precise, expressed unity. This careful scheme was carried through even later, when the original governing units were enlarged and new ones added.

◄ St. Mark's Square and the Doges' Palace

St. Mark's Basin, the Grand Canal and Giudecca Canal. In the foreground
the roof of the Doges' Palace and Cupolas of the Basilica

The Palace was the seat and established location of:
the private and public residence of the Doge, key figure
representing the new state, though the collegiate power
limited the exercise of his power more and more as
Venice grew; the Palace of the government, or City
Hall where Venetian political strategy was discussed
and settled in an assembly; the Palace of Justice where
the magistracies and the courts were seated, close by
the prisons; the Palace «ad jus reddendum» towards
the Piazzetta; the stables and living quarters for the
Palace servants and guards. Along the fourth side rose
the church or Ducal Chapel.

The Palace underwent other transformations, even
though they were only partial ones, enlarging it and
adapting it to changing needs. It is certain that as time
passed and the Republic became gradually more secure
and powerful, the architecture of the Palace lost its
original defensive function and, at the same time,
its fortress-like appearance, assuming the more open
forms of Veneto-Byzantine architecture. In 1106 the
ducal castle was damaged by fire; but it must have
been restored very quickly if, ten years later, it was

Façade toward the Basin. Ponte della Paglia in the foreground

sufficiently luxurious to welcome, with great pomp, the Emperor Henry V. The reign of the Doge Sebastiano Ziani was marked by a burst of energetic construction. In that period were executed such important projects as the filling of the Batario Canal and the consequent enlargement of St. Mark's Square. Even the Palace itself took on a new appearance and a new dimension between 1172 and 1178 with the construction of the new City Hall, to accommodate a larger Great Council Hall. Also enlarged were the Palace «ad jus reddendum» toward the Piazzetta, as well as areas for the other magistracies. In documents one finds many references to the halls of the Signori di Notte al Criminal, the «Advocatores comunis», the Quarantie, the Cataveri, the Piovego, etc.

But with the increasing importance of this most powerful Venetian institution, a decision was made about 1340 to build a new, grandiose hall for the Great Council. The larger room was necessary because of the gradually increasing number of the Council's membership and the growing needs of the body, which needed quarters which would also reflect the prosperity and strength of the ruling class. Thus the government final-

Northeast corner. Noah

View of the Quay. Library, Campanile and Doges' Palace

ly put an end to the indecision which had obstructed it previously, chiefly because some of those in power proposed only an enlargement and alteration of the old meeting hall. The new structure, in fact, was an extension of existing facilities, conserving those parts which were still useful and sufficiently strong to bear the weight of the new construction. Work was begun, as we have stated, shortly after 1340, under Doge Bartolomeo Gradenigo (1339—1343); it must have been completed almost entirely before 1365, since at that time the Paduan artist Guariento was summoned to fresco the wall over the throne with the «Coronation of the Virgin». Certainly work went ahead on the decorative areas like the vibrant lozenge-motif facing on the exterior, as well as the three-lighted, pointed arched great windows of the façade, all lost in the fire of 1577, excepting the last two on the right. The architectural structure of the large central windows was completed only in 1404. One is astounded at the speed with which the rulers of Venice planned and carried out this enormous construction project, especially if one keeps in mind the fact that work stopped from 1348 to 1350 because of a serious outbreak of the plague.

The building then reached toward the Piazzetta only as far as the sixth arch, or the seventh pillar from the Ponte della Paglia, corresponding to the width of the Great Council Hall. Only a few names of architects of the project are known; these appear in documents of the period: **Filippo Calendario** and **Pietro Basegio.** It is impossible to guess the identity of one single architect who may have been responsible for the design of this area. Documents also give the names of the three «Sapientes» (Experts) who were elected to study and oversee the construction. They were Marco Erizzo, Nicola Superanzio and Tommaso Gradenigo. In the course of their deliberations, they determined the location, size and shape of the new hall. In addition, they suggested certain brilliant ideas for the structure, such as the row of columns begun in 1348 down the centre of the Hall of the Piovego to reduce the length of the span overhead. The stonecutters and sculptors then in Venice working on the Palace must have made up a substantial corps of workmen, if they were able to finish so quickly not only the building itself but also the decorative elements such as the twenty-four capitals of the portico and those of the loggia, which number twice as many. The date «1344» is cut into the capital of the «Sapienti» on the tablet in Pythagoras' hand. A document dating from the end of this same year con-

Corner of the Piazzetta

firms that the ground floor and its portico and the floor above with its loggia were completed by that time. So was the wall of the hall itself, at least on the waterfront side, while the wall on the courtyard side was being built. It appears that the structural and architectonic concepts of the loggia's quatrefoil arches were absolutely revolutionary in that period in Venice. Doge Andrea Dandolo, an enormously rich and cultured man, certainly contributed much on an organizational and cultural level toward the development of the building and to its beautification. He spent a private fortune for the work done on St. Mark's Basilica as well as on the Palace.

Let us pause for a moment to consider the beautiful plastic solutions that decorate this part of the Palace and form the first important sculpture cycle. Unknown artisans inspired by new concepts and ideas worked their sculptures brilliantly into the architectonic whole; beginning at the corner next to the canal, there is «*The Drunkenness of Noah*», with his sons Shem and Japheth, while Ham is shown on the other end of the waterside arch. Above, at the height of the loggia, we find the *Archangel Raphael*, symbol of commerce, with Tobias.

At the corner toward the Piazzetta: «*Adam and Eve*», beneath the serpent's tree. Above, the *Archangel Michael*, with unsheathed sword, a symbol of war.

Looking ahead for a moment chronologically, mention will be made here of the sculpture at the third corner near the Porta della Carta (The Gate of the Paper): «*The Judgment of Solomon*». This superb marble group pays homage to Justice. The latest attributions made by art historians assign this to **Jacopo della Quercia**; it had previously been considered the work of **Pietro Lamberti**. Above stands the *Archangel Gabriel*, symbolizing Peace.

Another sculpture must be mentioned: the roundel which closes the seventh quatrefoil of the loggia and symbolizes «*Venice in the form of Justice*». Its style recalls the Noah and the Adam and Eve. As we have noted, the artists responsible for these sculptures and for the capitals remain anonymous, although one can perceive the hand of the many Gothic masters active around the middle of the XIV century. Perhaps Matteo Raverti actually worked on this project.

The central balcony of the façade facing the quay is the work of **Pier Paolo dalle Masegne**, dated 1400—1404. The statues in the niches represent St. Theodore and St. George (in an XVIII century copy), the Cardinal

Corner of the Piazzetta. Adam and Eve

Façade on the Piazzetta

Virtues, Ss. Mark, Peter and Paul. Crowning the whole is the statue of *Justice*, sculptured by **Alessandro Vittoria** in 1579.

Many of the capitals of the portico, both the more ancient ones toward the quay and the more recent ones on the Piazzetta, were substituted with replicas made during the extensive restoration of the Palace in the second half of the XIX century. The originals are kept in the Museum within the Palace itself. Here follows a rapid description of the subjects of these capitals, reading from the corner of the Palace at the Ponte della Paglia: 1) *Childhood and the Barber's Craft.* 2) *Birds.* 3) *Heads of Knights and Crusaders.* 4) *Childhood.* 5) *Heads of Emperors.* 6) *Female Heads.* 7) *Vices and Virtues.* 8) *Musicians and Monsters.* 9) *Virtues.* 10) *Vices.* 11) *Birds.* 12) *Vices and Virtues.* 13) *Lion's Heads.* 14) *Animals.* 15) *The Tournament of Love.* 16) *Male Heads.* 17) *Wise Men.* 18) *The Planets and the Creation of Man* (corner capital). 19) *Martyr Saints as Sculptors.* 20) *Animals with Prey.* 21) *The Trades.* 22) *The Ages of Man.* 23) *Peoples.* 24) *Marriage and Fatherhood.* Here ends the oldest series of capitals, dating back to the reconstruction of that part of the Palace which contains the Great Council Hall. As for

Façade toward the Basin. Central Balcony

the part built later during the reign of Doge Foscari:
25) *The Months of the Year.* 26) *The Tournament of Love.* 27) *Baskets of Fruit.* 28) *Vices and Virtues.* 29) *Virtues.* 30) *Vices.* 31) *Musicians and Monsters.* 32) *Teaching.* 33) *Vices and Virtues.* 34) *Birds.* 35) *Children.* 36) *Legislators.*

Some themes in this second series are duplicates of existing capitals. The last one bears the inscription «*Duo soti florentini inc se*». This refers to the two sculptors who created it; these two «*Florentine co-workers*» may be **Pietro di Nicolò Lamberti** and **Giovanni di Martino da Fiesole.**

The loggia facing the courtyard is quite different from the exterior. There are no elaborate, vigorous quatre-foils. Simple, pointed arches rest on two alternating types of grouped columns. They are: clustered columns of five shafts linked by the pedestal and the capital; and composite piers in groups of four columns attached to a central pilaster. The general feeling one gets from these is of something very much older than they actually are. One thinks more of the XIII century than of the XIV. The same may be said for the sculptured reliefs on the capitals which depict heads of people and lions. This more severe tone was in keeping with the

Façade toward the Basin. Portico Capitals

exposed massive brick wall beneath (intact until the restoration by Monopola) and with the two great walls of the Halls of the Great Council and of the Scrutiny, which are pierced only in the upper part by a series of small twin windows.

Finally the City Hall was completed. On it had been spent fabulous sums of money, and large sums continued to be spent for its maintenance. In fact, one single master artisan was named just to keep the paintings in good condition. At the end of the period of construction, the Republic decided to order payment of 1000 ducats by any aristocrat who proposed further restoration of the Palace. But Doge **Tommaso Mocenigo** (1414—1423) chose to forfeit this sum and proposed the reconstruction of the Ziani wing, which was certainly inadequate and probably in a state of ruin. One year later, when **Francesco Foscari** was elected doge (1423—1457), it was decided to restore the Palace of Justice, according to Mocenigo's proposal.

Between the two other buildings a passageway or portico must have existed, formed by the ancient walls of Istrian stone. It must, however, have been modified in the periods which followed. The planners or Council members themselves, who were always nominated in

Detail of a Capital

Portico on the Piazzetta

such moments, decided to go ahead with the Palace, extending it and using the same architectural solutions which had been adopted before. Thus the seat of government would appear as a single, expressive, architectonic unity. We have already seen that even the capitals of the portico and loggia were taken from XIV cent. models. We have no information about the masters who planned and completed the construction. They remain anonymous. In addition to the «Florentine co-workers» mentioned above, one finds evidence of Florentine taste in the part of the Palace next to the church. The influence of **Giovanni Bon** may perhaps be detected there; but the only name of which we are sure is **Giorgio Orsini da Sebenico.**

The Doges' Palace has two kinds of entrances: water and street portals. The water-entrances along the Palazzo and Canonica canals correspond to the landings inside the Palace. They are distinctive in appearance with their round-headed, twin-arched portals along the façade. The street entrance on the quay is through the Porta del Frumento (Wheat Gate) named for the Magistracy which obtained wheat for the city's granaries and worked close by. Another street entrance is the Porta della Carta, facing the Piazzetta, so-called be-

The Piazzetta. Columns of Mark and Theodore in the foreground

cause scribes and copyists worked near it. In addition there was a gondola landing for the Doge's apartment, in an area corresponding to the small courtyard inside, where two wells were located.

Before entering the Palace to begin the actual tour, here are a few more pieces of information about the building. The ground floor on the Piazzetta side was used for stalls, when horses were still ridden in the streets. Their use was eventually forbidden by law. The ground floor of the area nearest the water was used for prisons, eliminated finally at the beginning of the XVII century. Adjacent to the Walls, at the third landing on the canalside, Antonio da Ponte built, in 1568, the prisons called «The Gardens» because they were less severe than the older prisons, or perhaps the term was used... ironically. In 1601, these were pulled down. At the corner toward the Ponte della Paglia there still stood in 1500 the ancient tower which extended above the Palace roofline in the map of the city by De Barbari. Seven years later, it was demolished and the roofline was straightened. In this part of the Palace there also existed other prisons, called «The Little Tower», which were gradually eliminated to make room for the halls of the Armoury.

TOUR PLAN

Entering through the Porta della Carta, the visitor crosses the courtyard to the ticket-office, in the opposite corner, on the right. At the top of the Censors' Staircase there is the loggia, which one follows to the foot of the Golden Staircase. Two flights lead upward to the Gallery and then to the Doges' Apartment. This includes the Hall of the Scarlatti, the Map Room, Grimani Hall, the Erizzo Room, Hall of the Stuccoes (or Priuli Hall), Hall of the Philosophers, three rooms of the Painting Gallery and the Hall of the Squires. Exit onto the Golden Staircase again, where two consecutive flights lead to the second main floor. It contains: the Square Vestibule, Halls of the Four Doors, of the Ante-College, the College, the Senate Hall, the Ante-Chapel and Chapel. Crossing the Hall of the Four Doors once more, through a small passage, there are: the Halls of the Council of Ten, of the Bussola, of the Three Chiefs, of the Chief Inquisitor. Afterwards, one leaves through a narrow corridor and the landing of the Censors' Staircase. From here a stair leads to the Halls of the Armoury; the Hall of Gattamelata and of Henry IV, Morosini Hall and Bragadin Hall. Going down the Censors' Staircase, one enters the «Liagò», then the Halls of the Old Quarantia Civil and of Arms, also know as the Guariento Room, and the Halls of the Great Council, of the New Quarantia Civil, and of the Scrutiny or Ballotting. Continuing, one again crosses the Great Council Hall, and after walking through the gallery, one enters the Halls of the Quarantia Criminal and the Law Magistracy. One short wooden stair leads to the Bridge of Sighs, across the left-hand corridor. This point marks the beginning of the visit to the New Prisons, across the canal. The visit continues through a corridor which brings one back again to the Bridge of Sighs. Crossing it once more, along the second corridor, the visitor can see both the Basin of St. Mark and the Island of St. George through the marble grilles in the walls. Then one enters the part of the Doges' Palace intended for the Avogaria; from this little room, one can exit onto the loggia and end the visit to the Palace. On the same floor are the Hall of the Scrigno (or Coffer), the Hall of the Sea Militia, and that of the Doge's Seal. Returning once again to the small hall used by the Avogadori and to the Prisoners' Parlour, there is a small stair which leads to the prison cells on the mezzanine and those of the ground floor, called «The Wells». From here the visitor returns to the courtyard and ends his tour.

Corner at Porta della Carta. The Judgement of Solomon

PORTA DELLA CARTA

This is the main entrance to the Palace. The Most Serene Republic wanted an elaborate, unique architectural design for this portal. The available space was already clearly defined, wedged between a side of the church and the corner of the Palace. The position of the portal was determined by the existence of the medieval walls of the building, on which the builders very probably grafted the new structure. The commission for the work was given to **Giovanni and Bartolomeo Bon** on November 10, 1438. These artists enjoyed a great reputation at that time; and they must have worked feverishly in order to meet their commitments, not only to the state but to private individuals as well. This explains why work on the Portal was so often interrupted, regularly provoking the Council to appeal for its completion. In 1442, construction was in full swing. After the death of Giovanni Bon, his son Bartolomeo carried on alone until the gate was finished. He left his name carved on the architrave over the door: «OPUS BARTHOLOMEI». The gateway, taken as a whole, is an important example of mid-XV century flamboyant Venetian Gothic. This was the period when Gothic art was slowly giving way to the new Renaissance style, which came late to Venice and the lagoon, long after it had been accepted in Tuscany and Lombardy. The gate was ornamented not only with sculptures. We can now only imagine the polychrome painting in red, blue and gold, now lost, which enriched many areas of the portal. The apex is a statue of *Justice*. Until the end of the XVI century, it stood alone, white and gleaming against the sky. Because the staircase from the courtyard to the Hall of the Scrutiny crossed the Loggia of the Palace, it had to pass directly behind the statue, taking up a large amount of space. Thus the statue is now seen against a wall faced with designs in two contrasting shades, like the two façades. In the roundel below. a bust of *St. Mark the Evangelist* is crowned with a variety of architectural elements and decorative motifs, interspersed with leaf-scrolls and cherubs. This is perhaps by Giorgio Orsini. Below, along the two pilasters at the sides of the gate are statues in the round of *Charity, Prudence, Temperance and Fortitude*. In the central area, there stands a marble group with *Doge Francesco Foscari with the Winged Lion Passant*. This is a late work (1885) by **Luigi Ferrari,** a copy of the original. In the Palace Museum (Museo dell'Opera), the head of the Doge is preserved.

Museum of Sculpture. Marble head of Doge Foscari

THE ENTRANCE AND THE FOSCARI ARCH

Inside the Palace, one passes through the so-called
«Foscari Entrance» which leads to the Giants' Staircase.
This portico is roofed with a cross-vault, keystones of
which are sculptured figures of the Evangelists. This
work was presumably begun about 1438. Its overseer
was the Cremonese master stonemason **Stefano Bon di
Nicolò.** The project went forward under the new Doge
Cristoforo Moro, whose arms are in the final part of
the work completed. It was only around 1484, during
the reign of Doge Giovanni Mocenigo that the area
toward the courtyard was finished.

This is really one of the most confused areas of the
Palace, architecturally speaking. Many modifications
were made; they ended finally in the XVII century,
when Monopola built the small Clock façade, after the
demolition of the Foscari Staircase. This once led to
the loggia, and when it was pulled down, the passageway leading from the Hall of Scrutiny into the room
within the structural body of the Arch itself was also
destroyed. Other obstacles to a clear view are the va-

Foscari Arcade. Giants' Staircase in the background

rious changes made; modifications of taste during the years of construction, the fact that Gothic style was replaced by Renaissance style, and, finally, the fact that the architectural design and the decoration were made enormously difficult because of the location of the Entrance between the Palace itself and the side of the Basilica. Additional problems are encountered when one considers the confusion in attributing correctly the large number of sculptures on the many spires and fragile pinnacles of the structure. These statues, representing *Allegories of the Arts*, such as Science, Geography, Poetry, Music and so on, are attributed by modern critics to various artists from several cities of the Veneto and Lombardy. Among them is **Antonio Bregno**, responsible for the link between Gothic and Renaissance styles. Another is **Antonio Rizzo.** If we look from the upper landing of the Giants' Staircase toward the façade of the Foscari Arch, we are at once aware that the architect had a clear, whole concept in mind as he worked, and that he was in fact creating a splendid, open-air funeral monument destined to hold the body of the Doge Foscari.

The two lateral niches contain bronze copies of the two statues of *Adam and Eve* by **Antonio Rizzo.** The original marble sculptures are inside the Palace, in the Hall of the Quarantia. They are the most important works of late XV century Venetian sculpture, and the most meaningful expression of a great artist, architect and sculptor. In the past he has been too often overlooked by critics, thus a proper historical evaluation of him has been impossible until now. Rizzo was one of the first geniuses able to grasp and realize quickly the needs and demands of the new Renaissance style, which was reluctantly accepted in a city such as Venice, closely bound to the Gothic tradition and saturated with it. The statue of the *Standard Bearer*, in a niche in the small façade facing the courtyard, is also attributed to Rizzo.

Foscari Arch. Statue of Adam

Foscari Arch. Statue of Eve

THE LITTLE CHURCH OF SAN NICOLÒ

Giorgio Spavento, Procurator of St. Mark's, architect and structural technician, had built the little church of San Teodoro about 1486. In 1505, he was commissioned to do the *Little Church of San Nicolò*, in the corner of the Doges' Palace, facing the small courtyard of the Senators, which was created when a new wall was raised above the arcade already built by Rizzo. This small chapel is made up of one single floor with simple, round-headed windows, each crowned with a

Senators' Courtyard. Façade of the little Church of S. Nicolò

triangular tympanum. Spavento thus reached the height of the frieze of the nearby loggia. This he followed, using the same design of full roundels and festoons. When the building was finished, an elegant balustrade was added. This ornamented the terrace used by the Doge's family as a terrace-garden.

The construction took up very little time, though work went on after Spavento's death in 1509. It was **Pietro Lombardo** first and, later, **Scarpagnino,** who finished the paving of the courtyard as well as of the portico; they too are responsible for the building of the staircase called the «*Senators' Staircase*» which led from the ground floor to the loggia floor. The two large windows on the landing open onto the Courtyard of the Two Wells, behind the apse of St. Mark's. By 1515 the work in this area of the Palace must have been almost entirely finished.

THE EAST WING OF THE PALACE

In 1483, during the reign of Doge Giovanni Mocenigo, a fire broke out in the Doges' Palace. It first destroyed the Ducal Chapel and the Doges' Apartment, then ran through the east wing, causing serious damage to the entire structure. After the fire, the idea of demolishing the east wing and replacing it with a new construction faithful to the original design was rejected. This wing had been subdivided by various small inner courtyards which can still be identified from their placing along the canal-side. The Republic decided to preserve the existing building, so far as it was possible to do so. Restoration and reconstruction were assigned to **Antonio Rizzo,** who had been named Superintendent of the Palace shortly before. The architect projected a single, continuous structure with unbroken façades on the courtyard and on the canal. This, including the area intended for the Doge himself, reached upward to the eaves, including the second main floor where the Halls of the Senate and of the College were located. Lengthwise it reached as far as the corner of the structure where stood the Great Council Hall. Rizzo was not responsible for the construction; however, the unified architectural concept may well have been his. We know nothing of the previous appearance of the wing. One may be certain, though, that in its ground-plan it resembles the original, at least where the old building was sufficiently sound to be used.

THE GIANTS' STAIRCASE

Antonio Rizzo was also responsible for that splendid architectural and sculptural jewel, the *Giants' Staircase*. Its position was certainly suggested to Rizzo by the Signoria (Governing Body). An old plan was probably brought out to be carried through to its conclusion. The first concern was the direct connection between the ground floor and the loggia. This was the logical continuation of a plan already carried out in part in sections of the building then in use. The Porta della Carta, a vast Portico and the Foscari Arch were, in fact, mere episodes in the development of the building, rather than final steps taken. The portico inside the Porta della Carta leads the eye toward the point where the Giants' Staircase stands out in full view. The repeated intersection of the intermediate axes of these successive elements, terminating with the great arch of the loggia, forms a direct line ending at the top of the

Courtyard. Renaissance Façade (right), Foscari Arch and Giants' Staircase (background)

Giants' Staircase. This is a symbolic and actual route. Openings along the portico do not break up the long, shadowy space. This is followed by the Giants' Staircase, wedged in between the imposing façades of the fabric. It expresses perfectly a natural sense of swift, upward movement. At the top of the stair was the ideal place for the Doge's coronation. Here the ceremonies could be perfectly seen from below; dignitaries above could observe the crowd in the courtyard and on the loggias of the Palace. Quite beyond its architectural value, the Staircase has an interesting series of ornamental bas-reliefs along its sides, on its parapets and projections.

The two large statues which **Sansovino** placed here in 1567 are of Mars and Neptune. These are the «giants» which gave the staircase its name, though they are in fact incongruous and out of place because of their dimensions and their style.

Giants' Staircase, upper floor. Statues of Mars and Neptune

Courtyard. Renaissance Facade

36

THE RENAISSANCE FAÇADES

Work on the two façades of the east wing facing the canal and the courtyard was begun and continued simultaneously. We have fairly precise dates for the construction, which we can deduce from the coats-of-arms of several Doges which are part of the decoration of the façades. The canal-side façade was begun under Doge **Giovanni Mocenigo** (1478—1485); his arms are carved on the attached pilaster of the archway opening into the landing dock for the Doge's gondola. Next to

Renaissance Façade on the Rio di Palazzo

this begins the footing of the wall with its diamond-shaped ashlars. The façade toward the courtyard is of a later date. Built during the reign of Doge **Marco Barbarigo** (1485—1486), it bears his monogram on the first capital at the corner of the Senators' Courtyard. Work went on under his successor, **Agostino Barbarigo** (1486—1501). Both façades were built so rapidly that the seventh arch of the portico beyond the Giants' Staircase was reached at this time. The building already reached upward to the height of the first main floor, and its marble facings were also finished. At the same time, the internal structure was strengthened, so that by the date of Barbarigo's death, the interior was further advanced than the exterior.

We have precise records from the year 1498 about the unexpected flight of Rizzo from Venice, when it was discovered that he was guilty of embezzling the building funds. His successor was **Pietro Lombardo,** who had been working on the construction for some time and immediately took Rizzo's place as Supervisor of the Palace.

By 1514 the eleventh arch had been reached. Further along is the escutcheon of Doge **Francesco Donà** (1545 to 1553); from it, one concludes that work on the in-

Courtyard. Bronze Well

Courtyard. Clock Façade

terior façade went forward more slowly at this time, while on the side next to the canal the arms of Doge **Leonardo Loredan** (1501—1521) prove that construction progressed on this façade. After 1523, **Scarpagnino** also was active in the construction of the Palace. The completion of this massive restoration is owed to him, although Monopola was also involved in it at a later date.

On both façades the existence of older buildings is evident in the location of windows and sections of unbroken walls. One must admit, however, that these were used skilfully and intelligently. This is also noti-

Courtyard seen from the Giants' Staircase

ceable in the varying level of the stringcourses and in the long windows, which betray pre-existing Gothic forms. The same is true of the double cornice of the eaves, which matches the raised roof-level of the Halls of the Pregadi, of the College and of the Four Doors. After 1525 the *Censors' Staircase* was also built, to replace the external, open stairway leading from the ground floor to the second main floor. The date of its construction must be the same as that of the final work done on the rooms and the façade toward the courtyard (from 1525 to the middle of the century). This suggests that **Scarpagnino** was its builder.

Bartolomeo Monopola is one of the last architects who helped change the external appearance of the Palace. Taking up once more the design for the arches of the Renaissance façades, Monopola opened the unbroken walls which made up the two oldest sides of the courtyard. By doing this, he created a continuous portico. Between 1608 and 1615, he also built the small façade where the *Clock* is placed, attaching it to the bulk of the Foscari portico. This was done after the older, external stairway (called the «Staircase of Lead» from its leadplate facing) had been demolished.

The paving stones of the courtyard were laid in 1773, substituting older bricks. Along the long right band, formed by a simple design in Istrian stone, are two bronze *Well-Heads*. The first is by **Alfonso Alberghetti**, the second by **Nicolò de' Conti**. Both were done between 1554 and 1559.

THE LOGGIAS

The loggias are a most remarkable feature of the whole Palace. Extending along the full length of both external façades of the building, they face the Basin of St. Mark and the Piazzetta. The inner courtyard is also designed with loggias on three sides. Many offices of the government opened directly onto these, among them the offices of the Censors, the Avogadori, the Notaries, etc.

The builders of the wing which faces the Piazzetta located rooms only on the mezzanine of the structure. Thus they were free to use all available space for open expanses reaching through the Palace, from the external loggias to the inner ones. The only barriers were the transversal supporting walls; they are pierced with large portals. The loggia was named after Doge Francesco Foscari and called the *Loggia Foscara*, built during his reign.

Walking along the inner loggia from the Giants' Staircase, one sees many «Lions' Mouths», some of which still bear inscriptions identifying the magistracy in charge of accusations placed in them. There is also an elegant plaque designed by Alessandro Vittoria to commemorate the visit in 1574 of King Henry III of France. A second stone recalls the Papal indulgence granted by Pope Urban V in 1362. Here opens the portal of the Golden Staircase, easily seen because two free-standing columns, topped by statues in the round, flank it. These are by **Tiziano Aspetti**; they depict «*Hercules Slaying the Hydra*» and «*Atlas Supporting the Earth*».

Foscari Loggia. St. George Island (background)

LIONS' MOUTHS

In various parts of the Palace, along the loggia walls, in the Halls of the Bussola and of the Quarantia Criminal, are found Lions' Mouths. These were the special boxes built into the walls to receive secret accusations.

Interior of the Loggia toward the Golden Staircase

Lion's Mouth

DENONTIE SECRETE
CONTRO CHI OCCVLTERÃ
GRATIE ET OFFICII.
Õ COLLVDERÃ PER
NASCONDER LA VERA

The name comes from the custom of using a sculptured lion's head as an external decoration and its opening (the lion's mouth) as the slot where accusations were deposited. Every Magistracy had its own Lion's Mouth. There was one for the officials in charge of public vigilance; one served the office which punished petty crimes; another was for financial administrators. This system must certainly not have functioned well, at least when it was initially used, perhaps because it was not managed as prudently as in later years. In 1387, a law was passed decreeing all anonymous accusations invalid. It was thus necessary to sign the accusation and add the names of at least three witnesses. These names were to be kept secret; but if the accusations proved false, the witnesses would be prosecuted. Once the accusation was proved true, the Avogadori di Comun (State Attorneys) had the case reviewed by the Council of Ten before proceeding with it. Five consecutive ballots were necessary, together with a 4/5 majority in favour of prosecution, before further action was taken.

LA SCALA D'ORO OR GOLDEN STAIRCASE

After 1483, when a great fire destroyed the entire wing of the Palace along the canal, the Republic ordered a radical restoration of the building. This work went on for many years, even after the first half of the XVI century. Many rooms were completely rebuilt, and renovated. Others were added, with new corridors. The whole wing was altered, both in its ground plan and in its architectural structure.

At this same time, the arrangement of the stairways was changed to give better access to various halls of the Palace. Toward 1527, **Scarpagnino** built a wooden staircase between the Doges' Palace and the Palace of Justice. This made it possible to reach the Halls of the Pregadi and the College easily. In 1554, plans were made to rebuild this stair in stone. Three pairs of architects were asked to present designs. Among them were **Palladio, Rusconi** and **Sansovino.** Although Sansovino's design was ultimately chosen, the others' schemes received serious consideration.

The complex design of the Golden Staircase includes a single first flight of stairs with a double landing, followed by two successive flights. The right-hand flight turns back toward the courtyard, serving the storey where one finds the Doge's Apartment and the Halls of the Magistrate of Laws of the Quarantia Criminal. The stair then reaches the second main storey or third floor of the Palace, where the Halls of the Pregadi and the College are located. The arrangement is especially complicated. The actual construction was delayed at the start by discussions over its effectiveness. However, once the project was approved, work went ahead so rapidly that by 1558 the stair was completed as far as the Square Vestibule. The date of completion is carved there.

The decoration went ahead rather more slowly. It was finished finally in 1566. Artists responsible for planning and executing its splendidly rich decors are **Alessandro Vittoria,** who was originally commissioned to do it in 1559, and **G. Battista Franco.** To them we owe the beautiful vaulted ceiling and the white and gilt stuccoes. In the panels there are symbolic stucco figures in relief. Frescoes were also added. These same two artists also executed the staircase in St. Mark's Library while they worked in the Doges' Palace. The general theme is the

Portal on the Loggia of the Golden Staircase

Glorification of the Defense of Cyprus and Crete. On the upper flights of stairs, one may see *The Virtues Required of Good Rulers.*

In the first cycle the oustanding episodes represented are: *The Birth of Venice, The Coronation of the Queen*

Golden Staircase

of Cyprus, *St. Helen Before the Cross*, *St. Mark with Prisoners*, *Jove*, *Dedalus* and *Ariadne*.

The two statues in the niches of the second landing are *Abundance* and *Charity* by the sculptor **Francesco Segala.**

Golden Staircase. Vault decorations

Golden Staircase. Vault decorations

THE DOGE'S APARTMENT

From the first landing of the Golden Staircase, another short flight leads to the Gallery, a wide corridor dating from 1541. One end of it opens onto the landing of the Censors' Staircase, which leads to the Great Council Hall. At the other end, one enters the Doge's Apartment. This was rebuilt and decorated after the fire of 1483, first by **Antonio Rizzo** and later by **Pietro Solari**, known as **il Lombardo**. The work was done under Doge Giovanni Mocenigo and Marco and Agostino Barbarigo. In 1492, the rooms must have been ready for use, since Agostino Barbarigo moved into them in 1493.

THE HALL OF THE SCARLATTI

This hall was originally an anteroom for the Doge's Councillors.

Only the gilded wooden ceiling, with its blue background, remains from the original decoration. The design and carving are by **Biagio and Pietro da Faenza**, XVI century. The fee for this work was paid in 1506 by Doge Leonardo Loredan (1501—1521). The small fireplace between the two windows, bearing the Barbarigo crest, was designed and sculptured about 1507 by **Antonio and Tullio Lombardo**. Above the two doors are marble reliefs set in the wall. The first, of the Lombard school, represents «*The Doge Leonardo Loredan Kneeling Before the Virgin*»; the second, dated 1529, is by Paduan artists: «*Virgin and Child*».

Ducal Apartment. Room of the Scarlatti

HALL OF THE ESCUTCHEON OR THE MAP ROOM

The name of this hall comes from the fact that the escutcheon of the doge in power was displayed here. The arms now on the long wall are those of Lodovico Manin, last doge of Venice. The hall lies crosswise in relation to the Palace wing and extends through its entire width, from courtyard to canal. Facing both sides are rows of grouped windows opening onto balconies. This is the largest room of the Doge's Apartment, serving as reception hall and audience chamber.

The ceiling beams are painted; the walls covered with maps. This decor was originally finished about 1540 by the cosmographer **Giovan Battista Ramnusio,** a native of Treviso. Much later, in 1762, the original maps were replaced by those now seen. **Francesco Grisellini** was commissioned to do the work, which he finished quickly, with the help of his assistant, the painter **Giustino Menescardi,** who did the figures and lettering. Many countries representing all continents are to be found here: *Canada and Newfoundland; Arabia; Palestine and Egypt; France; Italy, Greece* and *Asia Minor; Iceland, Scotland* and *Scandinavia; Greenland; North and South America;* the *Cape Verde Islands;* the *East Indies* and *America; Asia.* At the center of the room are two large *globes* (XVIII cent.).

Ducal Apartment. Shield Room

LABRADOR
NOVA BRITANIA
Caroli
Fretal
P.Amilton

Albany

Mistani I.
SINUS
S. LAURENTI
TERRA
NOVA
Percy F.
Abitibi
L.
Sagueney
Anglorum
CANADENSIS REGIO
Quebech
MESSESAGII Nipifini L.
T.S.Petri
IROCENSES
Acadie
Halifax
Promontorium
Britanicum
Itologne
Corfu

NOVA ANGLIA
Boston
Areae I.
P.Cod
PENSYLVANIA
Coneticut
Nantucket I.
Albany
I.Longa
Philadelphia
Staten S.
MARILAND
Delaware
VIRGINIA
Chesapeak S.
Villamburg
Ban Town
Hatteral P.
CAROLINA
Lookout P.
Carlel Town Fear P.
Corteret P.
Sawanach
GEORGIA
FLORIDA
S. Augustino

OCEANUS
ATLANTICUS

Pram Floridae
CUBA I.

THE GRIMANI HALL

This hall is named for Doge Marino Grimani (1595—1606), whose family arms are in the centre of the ceiling. This is the first room of the Doge's Apartment. Salons and other rooms lie beyond. However, the loss of all furnishings and the lack of precise information about them make it impossible to know how the various rooms were used.

A very fine carved, gilt wooden ceiling on a blue ground dates from the end of the XV cent. or from the early XVI cent. The resemblance between it and the ceiling of the Hall of the Scarlatti would lead one to think that it too is by the **Da Faenza brothers.** That piece of information, in turn, allows us to date the ceiling sometime after 1504, when these two carvers worked in Venice. A frieze runs along all four walls. Made up of symbolic paintings, it was done by **Andrea Vicentino.** The figures represent *Venice, Architecture, Geography, Law,* etc. The fireplace, decorated with precious reliefs and elegant small columns, was done by the **Lombardos,** while the stucco mantelpiece was added, during the reign of **Pasquale Cicogna** (1585—1595). It bears his family crest. On the walls are two paintings attributed to **Gerolamo Bassano** (?). They are: *«The Ascent to Calvary»* and *«The Presentation in the Temple».*

Ducal Apartment. Grimani Hall

◀ Ducal Apartment. Shield Room. Detail of the Maps

Ducal Apartment. Erizzo Hall

Ducal Apartment. Stucchi or Priuli Hall

THE ERIZZO HALL

This hall is much like the room before it. The simpler ceiling maintains the same round decorative motifs. The gilt wooden carvings on a blue background were therefore done in the XVI cent. The fireplace is another work by the **Lombardos,** as are those shortly to be seen in other rooms. The overwhelming mantelpiece, an ornate and elaborate work in stucco, is out of balance with the whole. It bears the arms of **Francesco Erizzo** (1631—1646). The final arrangement of the furnishings is owed to him. The frieze, made up of a single, continuous canvas, was done between 1633 and 1638 by **G. Battista Lorenzetti.** It depicts *Cherubs* in various positions, as well as *Trophies of War.* One of the scenes alludes to the nomination of Erizzo as Head of Marine Supplies of the Republic. In addition to his crest, there are symbols of his power, such as his baton, his shield and, in the background, the poop of a warship. On the wall is a painting by an artist of the studio of **Jacopo da Ponte, il Bassano,** depicting the Biblical story of *Noah's Ark.* Animals of all species are grouped together in a large, barren area, waiting to be taken on board the miraculous vessel which will save them from the flood.

THE HALL OF THE STUCCOES OR THE PRIULI HALL

The Doge **Lorenzo Priuli,** who reigned from 1556 to 1559, first planned this hall, but little remains of the first decors. On the simple fireplace, faced with coloured marbles, are Priuli's arms. Those of **Pietro Grimani** (1741—1752) are set in the centre of the ceiling. At this time the room was completely transformed by the stucco ornaments on the wall and ceiling, which then took on its strange form of a ship's keel. The reliefs are made up of floral motifs and figures of caryatids. These are very expertly done. Paintings of various sources and of varying dimensions were then added.

By **Jacopo Tintoretto:** «*Portrait of Henry III*», painted in 1574 during the monarch's stay in Venice.

Giuseppe Porta il Salviati: «*The Ascent to Calvary*», «*The Meditation in the Garden*», «*The Circumcision*», «*Noli me tangere*» and «*The Holy Family*».

Leandro da Ponte, Bassano: «*The Adoration of the Shepherds*».

Antonio il Pordenone: «*The Dead Christ Supported by Angels*».

Bonifacio Pitati il Veneziano: «*The Adoration of the Magi*», painted about 1520.

THE HALL OF THE PHILOSOPHERS

This long room leads directly into the Map Room. Both halls together form a «T». At the far end, a row of grouped balcony windows open onto the small Courtyard of the Two Wells behind the apse of St. Mark's. The hall was used as a passageway and exit by the other rooms located beyond it on either side, thus repeating the design of Venetian patrician private dwellings.

The ceiling has painted beams, while the walls are decorated with XVIII cent. stuccoes of little importance. These were done under Doge **Marco Foscarini.** They frame canvases by an anonymous artist whose allegorical references are not clear. At once time they were displayed in the Hall of the Quarantia Criminal. These are surrounded by an extensive series of coats-of-arms of noble Venetian families. Also in this hall are full-length paintings of the doges *Vitale Michiel I, Vitale Michiel II* and *Domenico Michiel,* as well as a *«Holy Family»* by an unknown artist, dated 1637.

The first door on the right as one enters leads into the small staircase which was used by the Doge to reach the Senate and College directly from his apartment. On the inside wall over the door is the fresco of *«St. Christopher»* executed by **Titian** in 1524. The saint is shown crossing a flooding river.

Ducal Apartment. Hall of the Philosophers

Ducal Apartment. Hall of the Philosophers. St. Christopher by Titian

THE FIRST ROOM OF THE PICTURE-GALLERY

This is the first room of the Doge's Apartment on the canal side. As its original furnishings have been completely lost, the room was recently converted into a picture gallery. Its most outstanding feature is the cross-vault ceiling.

On the left wall is the painting by **Giovanni Bellini** *«Christ Mourned»*. Supported by the Madonna and St. John, the Body of Christ rises waist-high above the coffin. The high dramatic quality of the scene is achieved by such striking touches as the withered flesh of Christ, and by the anguished expression on His face. On the front part of the sepulchre is a small scroll where the artist signed his name: «IOHANES BELLINUS».

On the opposite wall is *«The Lion of St. Mark»* by **Vittore Carpaccio.** Painted in 1516, it shows the lion passant against a fascinating natural background of the lagoon and the Basin of St. Mark, with the Piazzetta, the Doges' Palace and the Basilica. A scroll bears the name of the artist and the date: «VICTOR CARPATHIUS A. D. MDXIV». Carpaccio was the first artist to present Venice in a townscape. Below is a row of escutcheons of Venetian patrician families.

A small wooden panel (XIV cent.) is by an unknown artist: *«Virgin Praying»*.

Ducal Apartment, Picture Gallery, First Room. Christ mourned by Giovanni Bellini (Detail)

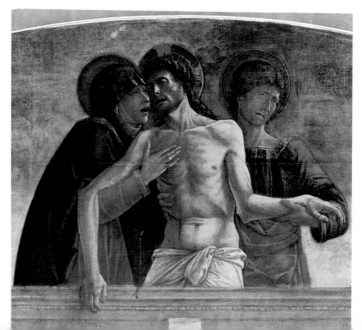

Ducal Apartment, Picture Gallery, First Room. The Lion of St. Mark by Vittore Carpaccio

The Lion of St. Mark by Vittore Carpaccio (Detail)

THE SECOND ROOM OF THE PICTURE GALLERY

In this hall are wooden panels by **Hieronymus Bosch,** painted in the first decade of the XVI century. These were once on display in the small passageway between the Hall of the Four Doors and the Hall of the Council of Ten.

They represent, respectively, «*Hell*», «*The Ascent into the Empyrean*», «*The Terrestrial Paradise*» and «*The Fall of the Damned*». The demoniac subjects are closely connected to the mainstream of Northern literature and legend of this period. These were directed to combatting diabolic manifestations which seemed obsessively ever-present. In these works, this trend is somewhat weak, and less than obsessive. Extraordinary is his concept of the Empyrean, made up of a dynamically foreshortened cylindrical opening with concentric luminous bands. At its farthest point, a brilliant light irresistibly attracts the souls of the elect.

Two other panels by Bosch are also worthy of the visitor's careful attention: «*Triptych of St. Liberata*» and «*Triptych of the Hermits*».

In the first of these, the central scene depicts the crucifixion of the saint, whose punishment was ordered by her own father, the pagan king of Portugal, who is perhaps the fat, indifferent onlooker in the foreground. On the left shutter of the altarpiece. one sees St. Anthony lost in deep meditation, while the background

Hell by Hieronymus Bosch (Detail)

◄Ducal Apartment, Picture Gallery, Second Room. The Triptych of S. Liberata by Hieronymus Bosch (Detail)

is crowded with demons. Hordes of people try to escape from a burning city. The right shutter shows a surrealistic landscape where a mass of broken tree-trunks and half-sunken ships protrude from the slimy waters of a seaport.

In the second triptych, the centre figure is St. Jerome praying in solitude; the lateral shutter portrays St. Anthony and St. Aegidius.

In this same room are shown two paintings of major interest. The first, by an artist of the School of **Enrico Bles, il Civetta**: «*Hell*». A city in flames is beset by hordes of ghastly demons from Nordic legends, part human, part animal. A horrendous slaughter is taking place. Sinners are being dragged away to eternal torment.

A work by **Quentin Metsys**: «*Christ Mocked*». In this painting, Christ appears as the ultimate expression of endless physical and moral suffering.

Ducal Apartment, Picture Gallery, Second Room. Christ mocked by Quentin Metsys

As for the room itself, all that remains of the original decor is the open-beam ceiling decorated with ornamental gold motifs and a precious fireplace by the Lombardos, between the windows. On it is the Barbarigo crest.

THE THIRD ROOM OF THE PICTURE GALLERY

Here, as in preceding rooms, the fireplace is of much interest. Designed and executed by **Antonio and Tullio Lombardo,** it dates from the early XVI century. This room is slightly smaller than those the visitor has just seen.

On the walls: **Boccaccio Boccaccino:** *«Madonna and Child»;* **Antonello de Saliba:** *«Christ Mourned by Angels».*

Leaving the third room of the picture gallery and crossing the Map Room, one enters the last room of the Doge's Apartment.

Ducal Apartment, Picture Gallery, Third Room. Christ mourned by Angels by Antonello de Saliba

THE HALL OF THE SQUIRES

This room is named for the squires, guards and other staff who protected the Doge.

Nothing remains of the room's original furnishings; it was re-decorated many times during the course of history, even recently. A rich, elaborate portal opens toward the Map Room. Several paintings from various sources have been hung on the walls. In the centre on an easel is «*Venice and Neptune*» by **Tiepolo**, formerly in the Hall of the Four Doors. There it could scarcely be seen because of inadequate lighting, having been hung over a row of grouped windows opening on the canal.

The paintings here were almost all done for the Offices of the Avogaria: **Jacopo Palma the Younger:** «*The Annunciation*».

Domenico Tintoretto: «*Venice, Faith and Three Avogadori with a Notary*». Also by Tintoretto: «*Doge Marino Grimani with a Committee of the Shoemakers' Confraternity*» and «*Doge Giovanni Bembo with the Guardian and Representatives of the Shoemakers' Confraternity, Before the Virgin*».

Pietro de Mera, il Fiammingo: «*Virgin and Child with Avogadori*».

Here ends the tour of the Doge's Apartment. We are again on the second landing of the Golden Staircase; its last two flights take the visitor to the second main storey, to the Square Vestibule. The tour continues from here.

Ducal Apartment, Hall of the Squires. Doge Giovanni Bembo and representatives of the Scuola dei Calegheri (Detail)

THE SQUARE VESTIBULE

This room was restored and its interior redecorated under the Doge Gerolamo Priuli (1559—1567). A new gilt wooden ceiling frames a **Tintoretto** painting of Priuli himself, set in the central octagonal panel. The walls were hung with precious red damasks, now lost, and were ornamented with four paintings, also by Tintoretto. These may now be seen in the Hall of the Ante-College.

The Square Vestibule is the entrance to the second main floor. Located at the top of the Golden Staircase, it has windows which open onto the courtyard. Here Casanowa spent the night in hiding, after escaping from the prison called «The Leads». At dawn, he was seen at the window and was fortunately freed by guards in the courtyard below.

The righthand doorway opens onto the **Hall of the Four Doors;** the small door on the left leads to a series of offices, staircases and **secret passageways** connecting the Halls of the Council of Ten and the Three Chiefs of the Inquisition; from there it goes also to the **Upper Chancery, Torture Chamber** and the very famous cells of **«The Leads».**

Behind the large door next to the entrance were located the only sanitary facilities in the Palace. In a small office were false cabinets, where toilets equipped with drain pipes were placed. Each small closet hat its own drainpipe leading outward through the wall; there were five in a row.

Square Anteroom. Doge Gerolamo Priuli by Jacopo Tintoretto

THE HALL OF THE FOUR DOORS

This clearly served as an antechamber. Here people were received and dismissed from adjacent rooms, whose four doors open symmetrically along the two side walls. These lead to the Halls of the Ante-College and the College, to the Senate and to the Hall of the Council of Ten. The last door, of course, leads one back to the Square Vestibule and the Golden Staircase. The row of grouped windows opens along the entire breadth of the end walls, thus making the room seem a passageway, which it was, rather than a living area.

The Hall was planned during the reconstruction of the entire Palace after 1483. The interior decors changed from time to time, but were altered after the fire of 1574.

The commission for the restoration and decoration was given to **Andrea Palladio,** while **Antonio Rusconi** supervised the actual work. The ceiling, with its barrel vault structure, is decorated with white and gilt stucco, a perfect expression of the sumptuous yet refined taste which Palladio brought to Venice, thus replacing the open-beam painted ceilings. The stuccoes themselves are by **Giovanni Cambi, il Bombarda,** while the «grotesques» were done by a certain **Maestro Baldissera.** The wall decorations were apparently completed at a later time, between 1595 and 1606, under Doge Marcantonio Grimani.

The portals, designed by **Palladio,** are each marked by two fine free-standing columns which carry the weight of a tympanum topped by three statues. Precious, rare marbles were used here, and the capitals were sculptured, according to modern authorities, by an artist called **Marcantonio,** who was then working in the studio of Alessandro Vittoria. The statues represent, respectively:

Door of the Square Vestibule: *«Secrecy»* (wrapped in a full cloak); *«Loyalty»* (holding a flute); *«Diligence»* (with pen and papyrus). All of these are by the sculptor and stucco-worker **Giulio Del Moro.**

Door of the Hall of the Council of Ten: *«Religion»* (with a crown of stars); *«Justice»* (with fasces); *«Authority»* (with sceptre); these are by the sculptor **Francesco Castelli,** a native of Lugano.

Door of the Senate Hall: *«War»* (armed); *«Pallas»*; *«Peace»* (holding an olive branch); the sculptor was **Gerolamo Campagna** of Verona (1589—1590).

Door of the College: *«Eloquence»* (with the moon and the caduceus); *«Vigilance»* (with a cock); *«The Gift of Speech»* (with a sparrow hawk), by **Alessandro Vittoria.**

Hall of the Four Doors

Hall of the Four Doors. Doge Grimani adoring Faith by Titian (Detail) ▶

THE PAINTINGS OF THE SQUARE VESTIBULE

On the ceiling, works by **Jacopo Tintoretto** and assistants: «*The Doge Gerolamo Priuli Receives the Scales and Sword from Justice*». In monochrome chiaroscuro: «*The Judgment of Solomon*», «*The Queen of Sheba Before Solomon*», «*Samson Defeating the Enemy Armies*» and «*Esther Before King Ahasuerus*». In the smaller panels, symbolic paintings of the four seasons.

The wall paintings were placed here in the XVIII century: Followers of **Paolo Veronese**: «*Christ Praying in the Garden*». By studio members of **Francesco Bassano**: «*St. John the Evangelist in the Act of Writing the Apocalypse*». **Gerolamo Bassano**: «*An Angel Announcing the Birth of Christ to the Shepherds*». **Paolo dei Franceschi, il Fiammingo**: «*The Expulsion of Adam and Eve*».

THE PAINTINGS OF THE HALL OF THE FOUR DOORS

The ceiling paintings are all by **Jacopo Tintoretto**. In the three central panels: «*Jove Gives Venice Dominion over the Adriatic*», «*Juno Bestows the Peacock on Venice*», «*Venice Breaks the Yoke of Slavery*». In the smaller oval panels Tintoretto represents symbolically the cities and regions subject to Venice: *Verona* (with its Roman arena); *Istria; Brescia* (with weapons); *Padua* (with books); *Friuli* (with plates and amphoras); *Treviso* (with sword); *Vicenza* (with the fruits of the earth); *Altino* (with ruins).

Along the walls, beginning with the wall of the Square Vestibule: **Giovanni Contarini**: «*Doge Marino Grimani Kneeling Before the Virgin*», painted toward the end of the XVI cent.

Titian: «*The Doge Antonio Grimani Kneeling Before Faith, and St. Mark in Glory*». This painting seems to have been begun by the artist as early as 1555. When Titian died in 1576, it was still unfinished. His nephew Marco Vecellio completed it in the years which followed, adapting it to this wall with two large figures on the sides. These are a standard-bearer and a prophet.

Giovanni Contarini: «*The Venetians Recapture Verona*», painted between 1595 and 1600. The episode took place during the war between the Venetian Republic and the Duchy of Milan, which was then ruled by Filippo Maria Visconti. The conquest of Verona came in 1439, when Venetian troops were led by Gattamelata, a mercenary captain. He is in the painting, in the right foreground.

Above, over the grouped windows is a photograph of

◄ Hall of the Four Doors. Henry III of France arriving in Venice by Andrea Vicentino (Detail)

Tiepolo's painting «Venice and Neptune», the original of which is in the Hall of the Squires in the Doge's Apartment.

Carlo and Gabriele Caliari: «*Doge Pasquale Cicogna Receives Gifts from the Persian Ambassadors*» (1590 to 1595).

Andrea Vicentino: «*The Arrival in Venice of King Henry III*«. This large painting documents Venetian life and customs. The many people in the canvas, the huge triumphal arch, designed by Palladio, all illustrate the details of this historic event. King Henry III of Poland, suddenly fled Cracow one night in 1574 to return to France to be crowned. One of the stops on his way was Venice, where he remained for some time, delighted with the magnificent celebrations organized by the Republic in his honour.

Carlo and Gabriele Caliari: «*The Ambassadors from Nuremberg Receive the Book of Venetian Laws from Doge Leonardo Loredan*». The painting, done between 1590 and 1595, shows part of the Hall of the College where this presentation took place, according to historians, early in the XVI century.

Over the grouped row of windows facing the courtyard:
Niccolò Bambini: «*Venice Supports the World*».

THE PAINTINGS OF THE HALL OF THE ANTE-COLLEGE

The octagonal ceiling panel: «*Venice Conferring Rewards and Honours*», painted by **Paolo Veronese** about 1578. The painting has often been restored.

The other oval panels were painted by **D'Angelo Marco del Moro** in monochrome. Symbolic themes represented are: «*Justice*», «*Navigation*», «*Abundance*», «*Meditation*».

In the frieze by **Francesco Montemezzano:** «*Silence and Fortune*», «*Jove and Pomona*» and «*Mercury and Minerva*».

On the walls are four splendid paintings by **Tintoretto**. These were once in the Square Vestibule, and were done between 1577 and 1578. They depict: «*Mercury and the Three Graces*», «*The Forge of Vulcan*», «*Pallas pushes away Mars*» and «*Bacchus and Ariadne*». The compositions, taken as a whole, are intended as the expression of the four seasons.

On the wall facing the windows, two other important canvases complete the decor of the hall. By **Jacopo da Ponte il Bassano:** «*The Return of Jacob*»; by **Paolo Veronese:** «*The Rape of Europa*» (1576—1580).

THE HALL OF THE ANTE-COLLEGE

This hall served as an antechamber for ambassadors and delegations waiting to be received by the Signoria. Here diplomats were ranged according to protocol; they readied the precious gifts which they were to lay at the Doge's feet. Here also gathered Venetian ambassadors, accredited at European and Italian courts, Rectors of mainland cities, Marine Supply Superintendents and naval officials returned from missions.

We have already mentioned that both the ground plan

Hall of the Antecollege

and the structure of the hall were clearly defined after 1483, during the construction which involved all of the Palace on the side next to the canal. The fire of 1574 again destroyed the Ante-College, which was restored at once. **Palladio** and his collaborator **Antonio Rusconi** offered a scheme which was different from that of the other rooms. The reduced dimensions of the hall and its different function suggested a vaulted ceiling, ornamented with stuccoes and frescoes, which was executed between 1576 and 1577. The superintendent of this work was **Antonio da Ponte.** Besides Palladio himself, other artists contributed to the hall. They may also

Hall of the Antecollege. Fireplace

have changed slightly the original projected design. Old documents name **Alessandro Vittoria, Tiziano Aspetti** and, above all, **Vincenzo Scamozzi.** The white and gold ceiling stuccoes were probably by the stucco-artist and painter **Marco del Moro.** He is also the presumed creator of the denticulated cornice and of the monochrome frescoes in the oval panels of the ceiling itself. The vast and elaborate frieze which covers the upper band of the walls is a later work.

On the window walls the fireplace with frieze and cornice clearly reflects the influence of Palladio. The two telamons, done in 1586, are among the finest works of the sculptor **Tiziano Aspetti.** The initials of the sculptor are to be found on the central relief depicting *«Venus at Vulcan's Forge».* The upper part of the fireplace is ornately decorated and perhaps even too elaborate.

Hall of the Antecollege. The rape of Europa by Paolo Veronese (Detail)

Vincenzo Scamozzi may have been responsible for it, having assumed part of the work as it was in progress. Observing the style of the fireplace stuccoes, one is led to believe that Scamozzi was also the designer of the ceiling.

The portal which leads into the Hall of the College was built of precious marbles: two free-standing columns sustain the architrave, which is decorated with festoons in relief. The cornice of the tympanum is surmounted by three statues by **Alessandro Vittoria.** These, done about 1576, depict «*Harmony*», «*Venice*» and «*Glory*». At one time the walls were hung with tapestries and gilt leather. These were replaced in 1735 with the four **Tintoretto** canvases painted about 1577 for the Square Vestibule and brought here with the **Veronese** and the **Bassano** canvases.

Hall of the Antecollege. The return of Jacob by Jacopo Bassano (Detail)

Hall of the Antecollege. Mercury and Graces by Jacopo Tintoretto

Hall of the Antecollege. Vulcan's Forge by Jacopo Tintoretto

Hall of the Antecollege. The Discovery of Ariadne by Jacopo Tintoretto
Hall of the Antecollege. Pallas driving away Mars by Jacopo Tintoretto

Hall of the College

THE HALL OF THE COLLEGE

In this hall met the magistracy known as the «Full College». It consisted of the Signoria, or Lower Council, made up of the Doge and his six Councillors; the three Chiefs of the Quarantia and the three «Zonte» (additional members) who were the Sages of the Council, also called the «Savi» or Great Sages. Chosen from the aristocracy, they remained in office six months. Also in the Full College were the Sages of the Mainland (five, elected every six months from the Senate); the Sages of the Orders (five, but not necessarily from the Senate). This last group had charge of sea power. This magistracy handled all preliminary discussion of matters brought before the Senate and managed the difficult negotiations with the Roman Church. It was also assigned a part of the powers of the judiciary, resolving controversies over benefits and advantages claimed by churches. Other matters treated were the privileges claimed by cities subject to Venice, customs charges and contracts. After 1526, the power of this unit grew rapidly; while it carried out apparently formal functions such as presenting official orders and decrees, it could withhold certain acts from the Senate, keeping them secret. Another function, generally public, was that of receiving and granting hearings to foreign delegations which came to Venice. These receptions always took place in the Hall of the College, where, on the raised dais of the tribune, the Doge and his Councillors stood, surrounded by the Sages, the Chiefs of the Council of Ten and the Grand Chancellor. The men received were important political and cultural figures, ambassadors, Papal nuncios, legates and Venetian patricians leaving for or returning from foreign assignments. These audiences often served to ratify old alliances and friendships or to sign new commercial treaties. Important agreements were thus confirmed in public at these highly formal, official ceremonies.

The hall, destroyed by the fire of 1574, was completely rebuilt in a short time. The speed with which it was done made possible the marked unity of style, which is all too rare in the Palace. The ceiling design, rich yet not too ostentatious; the architectonic structures; the furnishings and decors all seem to have been executed from designs by **Andrea Palladio.** His original plans date from 1575—1578 and were done in collaboration with **Giovanni Antonio Rusconi.** The gilt ceiling carv-

Hall of the College. Industry by Paolo Veronese

Hall of the College. Meekness by Paolo Veronese

81

Hall of the College. Sebastiano Venier after the battle of Lepanto by Paolo Veronese

ings, already completed by 1576, are by **Francesco Bello** and **Andrea Faentin.**

The artistic genius of **Veronese,** responsible for the magnificent cycle of ceiling paintings, adds one final touch to the stylistic unity of the room.

The wooden seats and tribunal are original. They are very different from those in other halls, which were restored in later periods. Outstanding are their elegant classical lines and mouldings, and the rich trabeation of the ducal chair. The cornices, the fluting of the columns and festoons are all finely gilded.

The rare marble fireplace between the windows was designed and executed between 1585 and 1595 by **Gerolamo Campagna,** who also sculptured the two statues, representing *Hercules* and *Mercury.* The historian De Zorzi attributes the chimneypiece to **Palladio** and the two statues to Campagna. The overseer of these works was the Palace Superintendent, **Antonio da Ponte,** who tended to both the execution of the works and to the choice of materials, as, for example, for the door leaves in cedar of Lebanon.

On the right wall, between the works by Tintoretto painted from 1581 to 1584, is the great wall **Clock** which matches that in the Senate Hall.

Hall of the College. Marriage of St. Catherine by Jacopo Tintoretto ▶

THE PAINTINGS OF THE HALL OF THE COLLEGE

The sections of the ceiling were all painted by **Paolo Veronese** between 1575 and 1577. In the central strip «*Mars and Neptune*», «*Faith, the Strength of the Republic*», «*Venice Enthroned with Justice and Peace*». In other panels are allegorical figures, each with its own symbol: «*Reward*» (sceptres and crowns), «*Moderation*» (eagle), «*Simplicity*» (dove), «*Dialectic*» (spider web), «*Meekness*» (lamb), «*Vigilance*» (crane), «*Faithfulness*» (dog), «*Prosperity*» (cornucopia).

Also by **Veronese,** the canvas on the wall above the throne: «*Sebastiano Venier's Thanksgiving for Victory after the Battle of Lepanto*». Also in the painting is the Superintendant Agostino Barbarigo, who died a hero in this encounter.

Over the entrance door, by **Jacopo Tintoretto:** «*Doge Andrea Gritti Venerating the Virgin*».

On the wall where the clock is located, from right to left:

Jacopo Tintoretto: «*The Mystical Marriage of St. Catherine, with Doge Francesco Donà Praying*», «*Doge Nicolò da Ponte Invokes the Virgin's Protection*», «*Doge Alvise Mocenigo Thanking the Redeemer*».

A series of monochromes completes the decoration of the hall. By **Jacopo Tintoretto:** «*Harmony*»; by **Veronese:** «*St. Sebastian*», «*St. Justine*»; by **Carlo Caliari:** «*Venice and the Virtues*», «*Politics*».

THE PAINTINGS OF THE SENATE HALL

In the middle of the central area of the ceiling is the large painting by **Jacopo and Domenico Tintoretto:** «*The Triumph of Venice*». The figure of Venice is set high above, in the clouds, surrounded by the Gods of Olympus; myriad divinities and tritons and nereids rise in an ascendant, whirling pattern bearing gifts and tributes to the city. In the two large ovals:

Marco Vecellio: «*The Superintendents of the Mint Oversee the Minting*» (above the throne).

Tommaso Dolabella: «*Doge Pasquale Cicogna Worshipping the Holy Eucharist*».

The other paintings: **Jacopo Tintoretto** (studio): «*Wisdom*»; **Andrea Vicentino:** «*Roman Warrior*»; **Andrea Vicentino:** «*Venus at Vulcan's Forge*» (lateral oval panel); **Andrea Vicentino:** «*Roman Warrior*»; **Marco Vecellio:** «*Liberty*» (?); **Marco Vecellio:** «*Allegorical Figure*»; **Andrea Vicentino:** «*A Philosopher*»; **Antonio l'Aliense:** «*The Doge Welcoming Historians and Poets*»; **Andrea Vicentino:** «*A Philosopher*»; **Jacopo Tintoretto:** (studio): «*Truth*».

Along the walls, a series of green monochrome figures in mock niches represent: «*Intelligence*», «*Equity*», «*Obedience*», «*Peace*», «*Justice*», «*Prudence*», «*A Philosopher*» (perhaps Ptolemy), by **Jacopo Palma the Younger.**

On the wall above the throne, **Jacopo Tintoretto** painted «*The Dead Christ Worshipped by Doges Pietro Lando and Marcantonio Trevisan*» (1590 ca.).

On the clock wall, in order:

Jacopo Palma the Younger: «*Doge Francesco Venier Presents to Venice Her Subject Cities*». The figures representing the cities bear symbolic gifts: Udine (vines and bunches of grapes), Padua (books, meant to symbolize its famous university), Brescia (weapons from its armourers), and Verona (wool).

Jacopo Palma the Younger: «*Doge Pasquale Cicogna Praying Before the Savior*». The woman's figure represents symbolically the island of Candia.

Jacopo Palma the Younger: «*Allegory of the League of Cambrai*». This alludes to the struggle which the Republic engaged in early in the XVI century against the major European states coalesced in the League. Venice soon lost all its possessions on the mainland and even the city itself was threatened from enemies close by. The diplomatically skillful Venetians succeeded in splitting the members of the League, chief among whom were Pope Julius II and Spain. After 1510, the Venetian armies reconquered all the lost territories. **Jacopo Robusti, il Tintoretto:** «*Doge Pietro Loredan Worshipping the Virgin*». The painting is a votive gesture for the cessation of the famine of 1569. Above the door: **Jacopo Palma the Younger:** «*Doges Lorenzo and Girolamo Priuli in Prayer Before the Redeemer*». Between the windows: **Marco Vecellio:** «*St. Lorenzo Giustiniani, Elected First Patriarch of Venice, Blesses the Crowd*». When the stalls flanking the throne were restored, **Gian Domenico Tiepolo** painted the two monochrome panels (1775): «*Cicero Accuses Catiline in the Senate*» and «*Demosthenes Accuses Aeschines*».

THE PAINTINGS OF THE VESTIBULE

Jacopo Guarana: «*Allegory of Good Government*» (fresco, 1777), «*Justice*», «*Dominion*», «*Science*», «*Fortitude*». **Sebastiano Ricci:** cartoon for the mosaic of St. Mark's Basilica illustrating *episodes in the life of the Evangelist*.

THE PAINTINGS OF THE CHAPEL

Jacopo Guarana: «*St. Mark the Evangelist amid Symbolic Figures of the Virtues*» (fresco, 1776).

Senate Hall

THE HALL OF THE PREGADI OR SENATE HALL

This magistracy was instituted in 1229. It originally was known as the Council of the Pregadi because its members were «prayed» by written invitation to attend its sittings. Only at the end of the XIV century do we begin to find in documents its other name: Senate. Then the number of members was fixed at sixty. They were elected annually. Later, other members were added, to make up the various «Zonte» or committees. These varied in number and were at first of a temporary nature, in time becoming permanent. Many members of other branches of government participated, like the Doge and his councillors, the magistrates of the Quarantia and the Council of Ten, the Avogadori di Comun and the Cataveri, as well as the Provveditori di Comun.

The complex, varied duties of the Senate were constantly augmented as time went on. Here were discussed the political policies of the Republic, especially deliberations concerning declarations of war. The Senate also named regular and special magistrates, such as the Superintendents, the Ambassadors and Rectors, not to mention the Patriarch, the Bishops and the prelates of subject territories. In addition, the Senate nominated committees to study new laws and projects concerning the administration of the State, its economy and its judiciary, its welfare and health, as well as the ecology of the waterways.

Toward the end of the second decade of the XVI century, it was decided to alter and finish decorating the Senate Hall. The architect **Scarpagnino** was named Superintendent of Works.

Some of the artists involved may have been: **Vittore Carpaccio,** at the beginning of the XVI century; **Giorgione,** whose fees were paid in 1507 and 1508, as we learn from period documents; and finally **Titian,** who certainly painted a «*Madonna Supporting the Dead Christ*» between 1554 and 1556.

This hall was badly damaged in 1574 by the fire which swept through the entire wing of the Palace along the canal. It was rebuilt and completely redecorated somewhat later than the rooms which precede it. Work was completed at the end of the century. The wooden stalls which one now sees here were restored again, in the XVIII century. In charge of the restoration was **Antonio da Ponte,** Superintendent of Works in the Palace. The artist **Cristoforo Sorte** of Verona designed the cei-

Senate Hall. Triumph of Venice by J. and D. Tintoretto ▶

ling in 1578. Its completion was delayed, however, until finally the Signoria dismissed Sorte. The large central panel is framed by broad, deeply carved volutes. Roundabout is a series of smaller panels, contained within the lateral band.

The paintings were also done between 1581 and 1595. The original scheme, later abandoned, provided for setting the huge «Chorography of the Venetian States» along the walls. This was to have been executed by the decorator Cristoforo Sorte, who was also a competent cartographer. On the wall facing the windows are two large wall clocks whose faces are decorated with signs of the zodiac and symbols of the phases of the moon. The Senate Hall is directly connected to the Halls of the College and of the Four Doors. Two small lateral doors at the sides of the throne lead respectively to the

Senate Hall. Doge Francesco Venier presents Venice with the subject cities by Jacopo Palma the Younger (Detail)

Senate Hall. Doge Pietro Loredan adoring the Virgin by Jacopo Tintoretto

VESTIBULE AND SMALL CHAPEL

In these two rooms was a collection of museum curiosities, bequeathed to the Palace by Domenico Grimani. In 1593 they were transferred to the St. Mark's Library. Thus these two rooms were adapted to their present use.

On the **Vestibule** wall facing the entrance are two doors. That on the left led to the Office of the **Chief Cashier;** from there a passageway led to the **Banquet Hall,** located in the building used by the Canons of St. Mark's. This building is now part of the residence of the Patriarch of Venice. These passageway no longer exist. Through the other door one reached the former chapel, later remodelled with other rooms destined for the **Secret Archive** of the Republic. In 1770 several paintings were hung in the Vestibule. Only one remains: the cartoon by Ricci for the mosaic of St. Mark's.

While Pasquale Cicogna was still Doge, **Scamozzi** set up the **Chapel** on the altar of which was placed the interesting sculpture by **Jacopo Sansovino** of the «*Madonna and Child*». The paintings are by the perspective artists **Agostino and Gerolamo Mengozzi-Colonna,** collaborators with **Jacopo Guarana,** who painted the ceiling fresco. The stairway besides the altar leads directly downward into the Doge's Apartment.

Antechapel. Cartoon by Sebastiano Ricci

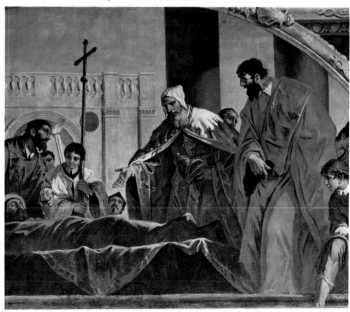

Chapel. Madonna by J. Sansovino ▶

OPVS · IACOBI · SANSOVINI · FLORENTINI

THE HALL OF THE COUNCIL OF TEN

The Magistracy which sat here was instituted in 1310. In this year Baiamonte Tiepolo plotted with others to overthrow the government. Thus Magistrates were named to judge and pass sentence on the conspirators. Afterwards this body watched over state security, although it existed only on a temporary basis.

It became permanent in 1455, under a Great Council decree. Formed of ten members elected annually from the Senate, it also included the Doge and his six Councillors. A State Attorney or Avogadore was also present at its sittings, with the veto power. He could also accuse any member of the Council of Ten who might have committed an illegal act. The functions of the Council were many; often very delicate matters were handled. A branch of the police, it had jurisdiction over political and criminal matters. It judged such offenses as treason and espionage, and was delegated to safeguard the wellbeing of the citizenry. All duels and violence against private citizens fell under its competence, as did all affairs involving the use of weapons. It guarded public morality and controlled public holidays and celebrations. The Council even ruled on fashions in dress. Custody of the Palace Armoury was given to it; and

Hall of the Council of Ten

Hall of the Council of Ten. Elderly Oriental and Young Woman by
P. Veronese

the Council was also protected by special armed guards. It had its own separate treasury, which it controlled. Such authority often led the Council of Ten to invade areas where it had no right to interfere, such as administration, finance and even foreign policy.

Toward 1516, **Scarpagnino** completed the restoration of the hall, left unfinished by **Pietro Lombardo.** The decoration was done in the middle of the XVI century. The wooden ceiling was finished in 1553, and its general design appears simple. It is subdivided into compartments by richly carved, gilded cornices.

The paintings were assigned to **G. Battista Ponchino,** who chose the young **Veronese** as his helper. Veronese, in turn, wanted to work with his own student **Zelotti.** The themes of the canvases, suggested by the scholar **Daniele Barbaro,** are symbolic.

The original furnishings are partly intact, though the seats or stalls are missing from the semicircular tribune. Off it opens a small, secret door leading to the little offices on the mezzanine and to the dark, narrow stairs which communicate with the cells beneath the roof, the Leads, and those on the ground floor, the Wells. This staircase was used to transfer accused persons to and from the torture chambers and prison cells without leading them through the public areas.

PAX ITALIÆ BONONIÆ

THE HALL OF THE BUSSOLA

This hall takes its name from the wooden entrance screen in the corner to the right of the door. It conceals a double portal leading to the Hall of the Three Chiefs of the Council of Ten, as well as to service passages. The hall is a focal point in the ground plan. In fact, besides giving access to the two halls of the tribunals, the Hall of the Council of Ten and the Hall of the Three Chiefs, it communicates directly with the Censors' Staircase. A painting by the XVIII century artist Bella shows this room full of people waiting to be received by members of various high government councils. The figures represent witnesses, accusers, the accused and defenders. The hall, then, was a vestibule.

Here, too, the decorations were restored towards the middle of the XVI century (1550—1555). In addition to the bussola, the decors include the wooden seats and the fireplace between the two windows. It was completed from a design by Jacopo Sansovino by the artist's own pupils Danese Cattaneo and Pietro da Salò, who did the two telamons. The arms of Doge Marcantonio Trevisan (1553—1554) are sculptured. Beside the door there is the only remaining Lion's Mouth, or letter-box for accusations, remaining intact, with its two small wooden doors complete with two locks.

◀ Hall of the Council of Ten. Peace Treaty of Bologna by M. Vecellio (Detail)

THE PAINTINGS OF THE HALL OF THE COUNCIL OF TEN

The ceiling is made up of 25 panels of various shapes. The recurring theme, conveyed symbolically, is the concept of Good Government, accompanied by the Power of the Republic.

G. Battista Zelotti: twelve panels in green monochrome, triangular in general form, though using both straight and cuved lines for their frames, represent the *Months* of the year. This same artist painted the four women's figures in monochrome, symbolizing the *Morea, Candia, Cyprus* and *Venice.*

In the center, a work of **Andrea di Jacopo,** *«Jove Descends from the Sky to Strike Down the Vices».* This is a copy of the famous Veronese painting which the French removed in 1797.

The four oval panels are, respectively, the work of

G. Battista Ponchino: *«Neptune in a Chariot Drawn by Sea Horses».*

Paolo Veronese: *«Old Oriental Man and a Young Woman».* This work has an extraordinary pictorial quality and vividness. The composition, even within the constricted oval form, achieves a perfect balance of surface and volume. Its colour is fine, and brilliantly luminous. The theme seems to allude to the Old and Young States.

G. Battista Zelotti: *«Venice Seated on the Globe, and the Lion of St. Mark».*

G. Battista Zelotti: *«Janus and Juno».* The symbolism probably refers to the prudence of the Council of Ten.

In the four rectangular compartments:

G. Battista Ponchino: *«Mercury and Minerva».*

G. Battista Zelotti: *«Woman's Figure in the Act of Breaking Her Chains».*

Paolo Veronese: *«Venice Receives the Doge's Cap from Juno».*

This, too, was taken away by Napoleon and sent to Belgium in 1797. It was given back to Venice in 1920.

G. Battista Zelotti: *«Venice Between Mars and Neptune».* The theme is clearly the exaltation of the naval and military power of Venice, as symbolized by Venus.

On the walls beneath the frieze (where a series of cherubs alternating with mottoes are playing as they carry weapons, flags, amphoras and play musical instruments) from right to left:

Francesco and Leandro da Ponte, Bassano: *«Pope Alexander III Meets Doge Sebastiano Ziani After the Battle of Salvore».* The painting, begun by Francesco and completed by his brother after 1592, recalls one of the historical events amply illustrated by the paintings in the

Hall of the Great Council, to which we refer the reader.

Antonio Vassilacchi l'Aliense: «*Adoration of the Magi*».

Marco Vecellio: «*The Peace of Bologna*». In the center, Clement VII and Charles V, who met in Bologna in 1529 to sign a treaty. Many Italian states were represented at this historic meeting, the Republic of Venice among them. The main square of the city and the Church of St. Petronius are seen in the background, to the left of the throne.

THE PAINTINGS OF THE HALL OF THE BUSSOLA

The octagonal central panel in the ceiling, «*St. Mark in Glory*», is a copy by **Giulio Carlini** of Paolo Veronese's original. This, too, was removed by Napoleon. The Veronese is now in the Louvre.

The other twelve ceiling canvases, done in chiaroscuro in green monochrome, represent historical allegories. By artists of the School of Veronese, they depict triumphal processions and winged figures.

On the walls above the seats, on the right as one enters:

Antonio Vassilacchi l'Aliense: «*The Conquest of Bergamo*». This episode dates from 1427, while the Republic was at war with Filippo Maria Visconti for dominion over the Italian mainland.

Marco Vecellio: «*Doge Leonardo Donà Adoring the Virgin*». Signed «Marcus Titiani» by the artist.

Antonio Vassilacchi l'Aliense: «*The Conquest of Brescia*». This depicts another episode in the war against Filippo Maria Visconti.

THE PAINTINGS OF THE HALL OF THE THREE HEADS OF THE COUNCIL OF TEN

G. Battista Zelotti: «*Virtue Conquers Vice*», in the octagonal centre panel. In the larger rectangles are symbolic figures alluding to the acts and decrees of this Magistracy.

Paolo Veronese: «*The Forger Punished*».

G. Battista Ponchino: «*Justice Conquers Rebellion*».

Paolo Veronese: «*Victory Conquers Sin*».

G. B. Ponchino: «*Sacrilege Thrown into the Abyss*».

THE PAINTINGS OF THE HALL OF THE CHIEF INQUISITOR

The octagonal panel on the ceiling is the work of **Tintoretto**. Its subject is «*The Return of the Prodigal Son*». In the rectangular panels, figures of women representing «*Faith*», «*Law*», «*Justice*» and «*Harmony*». These are by Tintoretto or by artists from his studio.

Hall of the Three Chiefs of the Council of Ten

THE HALL OF THE THREE CHIEFS OF THE COUNCIL OF TEN

Here was seated the Magistracy which originated in the Council itself. At first, before 1539, it was considered a supplement of the Council. From the time the Inquisition was instituted, these men were elected regularly each year by secret ballot. Two of them were chosen from the Ten; the third, from the Doge's Councillors. From the colours of their robes they took their names: «The Blacks» for the men from the Council of Ten; «The Red» from the man from the Doge's Council. The specific area of duty was repressing acts against the State. Included were treason, disclosure of state secrets, espionage, speaking against the government and having close friendships or long contacts with foreigners. The Inquisitors supervised the archives of official reports and journals kept by ambassadors and rectors; chiefs of the Council checked the integrity of magistrates, while aristocrats and common citizens were also under their surveillance. An efficient network of informers served them, making this Magistracy one of the most feared government agencies.

The restoration of the Hall was begun by **Pietro Lombardo** and continued by **Scarpagnino** after 1516. The Hall is not refurnished and the original paintings are missing. They are by **Zelotti, Ponchino** and **Veronese,** executed between 1553 and 1555. The themes refer to the functions of the Three Chiefs of the Council.

Jacopo Sansovino designed the fireplace, while **Danese Cattaneo** and **Pietro da Salò** sculptured the two telamons. The sculptured arms are those of Doge Marcantonio Trevisan.

THE HALL OF THE CHIEF INQUISITOR

The small room which follows, called the Hall of the Chief Inquisitor, was most probably the office of the Doge's Inquisitorial Councillor, head of the Three Chiefs of the Council.

This hall, like many others, has been completely changed over the centuries. It has lost its precious gilded leather facings; its ceiling was restored. In the centre is **Tintoretto's** «*Return of the Prodigal Son*». The two halls communicate directly with the Hall of the Council of Ten and with the prisons.

Hall of the Chief Inquisitor. Return of the Prodigal Son by J. Tintoretto

THE ARMOURY

The Venetian Republic, always careful to maintain its political stability, had found it necessary to keep a deposit of arms inside the Palace itself. Thus any unexpected assault from outside could be faced at once. It is certain that as far back as the XIII century and perhaps even earlier, there existed an armoury in the Palace. The Council of Ten was designated caretaker of this armoury, which was called the «Munition». The importance which the Council attributed to it is convincing evidence that the war materiel kept here was very expensive. The possession of arms, a decisive and readily available source of power, was also an uncommon prerogative. In the hands of the State, it assured the Republic a certain security and tranquillity. The weapons, depending on the various historical periods during which they were acquired, were amassed in very large numbers, in series according to type and were absolutely practical; hence, for everyday use in combat.

In the course of time, other purely decorative weapons and parade arms were added to this collection. There are also precious trophies and curiosities, the results of peace treaties, alliances and booty. One document of 1317 names the exact place where the Armoury was located: near the former Great Council Hall.

After that date, its location was often changed, either because more space was needed or because safer quarters seemed necessary. Toward 1532, provision was made to move the Armoury for the last time, into the rooms which are used for it today. In 1609 another room was added, on the floor below, near the Hall of the Great Council. Formerly known as the Hall of Armament, it is now the Hall of Guariento. Here arms were kept always loaded and at the ready during all the councils.

Access to the Armoury was prohibited to all excepting the Chief of Munitions, who got the keys each day from the Secretary of the Council of Ten. Sometimes the Armoury was visited or perhaps checked by persons in authority, but this was done only after special deliberation, and even then the controlling official was accompanied by Council members. They were obliged by law to check the arms periodically and inspect them fully to guarantee their perfect functioning. Only very rarely was any part of this Armoury distributed to the active militia, as in 1570 during the war with Candia. The fall of the Republic marked the partial dispersion of this precious collection. Regardless of the fact that

Hall of Gattamelata. Equestrian Suit of Gattamelata

Venice was sacked, and in spite of thefts after 1797, the collection shown here is still rich and impressive. The Armoury today consists of 2031 pieces divided into various types: sidearms and firearms, arms for offence and defence, arms for combat, for jousts and parades. There are *halberds; pikes* and *ranseurs; falchions* and *battle-axes; hammers; conventional swords; broadswords; long rapiers; rapiers; daggers; spiked maces; bucklers; spiked shields; targes; brigandines; helmets; morions; armours; bows; catapults; quivers; field insignia and banners; standards;* and *commanders' insignia.*

THE FIRST HALL, OR HALL OF GATTAMELATA

The *equestrian armour* on the dark horse has been known for centuries as *Gattamelata's,* since it apparently belonged to the celebrated condottiere and soldier of fortune, Erasmo da Narni, Commander in Chief in the pay of the Republic from 1433 to 1442, the year of his death. This armour is certainly the work of Italian craftsmen, attributable to Brescian armourers. Complete in every particular, it has a helmet with gorget, a visor with double sights, tassets and cuishes which are skilfully articulared with swallow-tail linkage. On the breastplate and kneecaps, which are gilded and embossed, is a group of animal heads; at the centre a cat, and on the sides the profiles of two wolves.

The second set of *armour* is by Venetian XVI century craftsmen; it belonged to Senator **Francesco Duodo.** The *dog-face type helmet* to the left of the door is probably the work of Italian armourers dating from the first half of the XIV century. Extremely rare in both its style and workmanship, its helmet and gorget are worked from a single piece of metal. In ancient documents, it is called «*Attila's Visor*».

Hall of Gattamelata. Beaked Sallet

Hall of Henry IV of France. Armour of King Henry IV of France

Hall of Henry IV of France

THE SECOND HALL OR HALL OF HENRY IV

Here are found several pieces of exceptional artistic and historical value:

In the centre, a large *culverin*, with nine ounce gauge, complete with its framework in walnut, with original decoration and rigging. The piece is covered with bronze reliefs and interlacing floral motifs; its mouth is the head of a fantastic dragon, while on the muzzle is a full-relief group showing a soldier killing a dragon. This is Italian, from the first half of the XVI century, attributable to **Alberghetti,** a armourer of the period.

A *«Match»* urn, for arquebus, of embossed copper fretwork. The piece is signed and dated: **GB Comino** 1621. The vessel, whose cover is shaped like a cupola, contains sufficient apertures for 106 firing matches. Similar ones were used on Venetian warships.

The *Turkish Standard* from a warship, on the ceiling, is probably part of the booty taken during the Battle of Lepanto.

Several big, *two handed swords*, with teeth on the forte, may be seen on the rack on the wall. Two bear the signature of a famous family of swordsmiths from Belluno: **Giorgio and Giuseppe Giorgiutti.** The grip is covered with turtle skin and white ivory. The initials of the Council of Ten and the Lion of St. Mark are engraved below the pommel.

Of the three *horse chamfrons*, the first, painted black, is larger than the others and can perhaps be dated from the XVI century. The second, with a raised frontal rose and spike, seems to have been a gift of Henry IV of France to the Republic. The third, with protruding blinders and a spiral braid down the front, belonged to Colleoni. The attributions are all taken from old inventories.

The Armour of Henry IV of France, gift to the Republic in 1603, has the simple, smooth lines of battle armour. It bears the mark of the trial blow struck upon it before it was released from the workshop. On the breastplate is the engraved golden badge of the Order of the Holy Spirit. The political importance of this gift led the Venetian Republic to place the royal armour in a special niche.

The two combined thrusting and fire arms of halberd type are very rare examples of their kind. They conceal in their shafts the barrels of an arquebus. Another interesting example is *the complete armour of a youth,* dating from the first of the XVI century. It is said to have been found on the battlefield after the Battle of Marignan (1515).

Hall of Henry IV of France. Fuse Urn by G. B. Comino

Morosini Hall

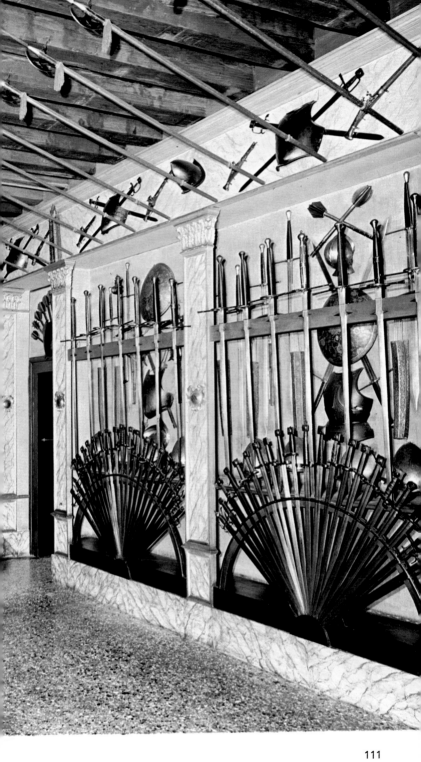

THE THIRD HALL OR HALL OF THE MOROSINI

This hall still has the original arrangement of the XVII century, as it appears in a painting of that period and in numerous prints. On the far wall is the bust of **Francesco Morosini,** the celebrated Venetian admiral known as The Peloponnesiac. This is by **Filippo Parodi,** pupil of Bernini.

Among the pieces on display, most important are the *two cuirasses with tournament helmets* from the second half of the XV century. Both bear on their right shoulder the engraved emblem of the Sforza family, three rings intertwined, with the initials «A. M.». These are attributed to the **Missaglia,** a famous family of Milanese armourers in the service of Ascanio Sforza. Of the two, the most complete is on the left; it weighs a full 23 kilograms. These were fabricated with the care necessary to make them invulnerable to blows of lances and maces, provisions never taken for combat armour.

Another precious piece is a *muzzle-loading arquebus,* with twenty barrels, long and short, fitted into a revolving cylinder. The weapon, interesting above all from a technical point of view, is mounted on a fixed base; it turns on a pivot which permits it to fire in all directions. The work dates from 1571, by **G. M. Bergamin.**

THE FOURTH HALL OR HALL OF THE ARQUEBUSES

This room was dedicated to **Marcantonio Bragadin,** whose bust in bronze is the work of **Tiziano Aspetti.** At the center of the hall near the window is *a small cannon or mortar with cylindrical breech and five revolver-type barrels.*

In this hall are assembled various series of arms of different types:

the so-called «white arms» such as *swords, small swords, daggers, epées* and *rapiers* of many kinds and makes. A Venetian sword called an *ox's tongue,* derived from the ancient «cinque dea», *Venetian sword* of the XV century with the arms of the **Pesaro** family on its ricasso; other XVI and XVII century swords, bearing curious mottoes on their blades: PIPPO MI FE; VINCIT AUT MORI; SI DEUS PRO NOBIS QUIS CONTRA NOS; JESUS MARIA, and so on. Besides the marks of renowned Italian and foreign armsmakers, one finds engraved the names of craftsmen of equal fame such as **Antonio Piccinino** on a perfectly balanced blade; or

Morosini Hall. Jousting Sallet

Hall of the Arquebuses. Buckler

Hernande and Tomaso en Toledo on a sword and small sword of the XVI century.

Firearms such as *arquebuses, pistols, light pistols.* The arquebuses are of Italian, European or Oriental origin. Those from the East are mostly Persian, certainly a gift to the Republic from ambassadors and emissaries. A wheel-lock arquebus with a three-shot repeater mechanism is a work of the second half of the XVI century, signed **Giorgio Bergamin.**

Two *flint-lock rifles* from the first half of the XVII century are hunting weapons from Poland. The long steel barrel, the breech and stock are ornamented in relief with *battle scenes and the story of the Prodigal Son,* surrounded with interlacing branches and leaves. A *small revolving cylinder arquebus* of the late XVI century, signed by **Lazzaro Cominazzo.** *Wheel-lock pistols* of Silesian origin (Teschen, 1625). Short *double-barrelled pistols* with the barrels mounted above and below the central case; the case and stock are in carved ivory. Short, *wheel-lock pistol* with barrels above. Small *pistol with three barrels* welded together on a revolving cylinder.

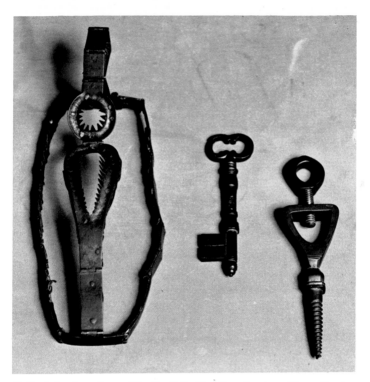

Hall of the Arquebuses. Chastity Belt, Dart-throwing key, Finger Crusher

Among the various other weapons, the pointed arms, staff weapons, projectile arms and firearms, one finds: two *steel axes* with firing barrels hidden in the handles; one *sabre* with the firing barrel in the rib of the blade; four *cross bows* with their firing barrel fixed to the shaft. One of these bears the carved signature of its maker and the year of its manufacture: **Renaldo da Visin da Asolo,** 1562.

One should also notice the series of peaked, crested *morions,* the *bucklers* and the *brigandines.*

Other arms and curious instruments are: a steel *crossbow* 25 centimeters long; an *iron key* provided with a spring to shoot a little poisoned dart; and finally a *chastity belt,* listed in old inventories as: «*iron pants of the wife of the Lord of Padua*».

At the bottom of the short flight of stairs which leads to the Censors' Staircase, one may note the lock of the Armoury door with the initials of the Council of Ten: «C. X.». A false secret nailhead releases the lock, letting the key turn. The Censors' Staircase leads to the first main floor or floor of the Great Halls.

PASSAGEWAY OF THE GREAT COUNCIL AND VERANDA (LIAGÒ)

The word «liagò» in Venetian dialect means «veranda». The Vestibule and Liagò are joined to form a single, L-shaped room; the huge windows with pointed arches facing the Basin of St. Mark still conserve their quatrefoil marble lights, lost in the rest of the building in the fire of 1577. The hall served as an antechamber during the sittings of the Great Council.

The passageway still has its open-beam ceiling, painted and gilded at the end of the XVI century. Along the right wall, between two large doors which open onto the Great Council Hall, the stalls are very elaborate; they were returned here. On the left, beyond the great archway of the Censors' Staircase, one finds the Halls of the Quarantia Civil Vecchia and of the Armament, now changed, which contains the Guariento fresco.

HALL OF THE QUARANTIA CIVIL VECCHIA

The Quarantia was instituted perhaps in 1179, but it took definite form later, at the beginning of the XIII century. It is named for the forty members who formed it. This Magistracy was the supreme court of appeals for all sentences passed by the Magistrates of the City, the dukedom, Dalmatia and other distant dominions. Its specific duty was, however, the issuing of sentences in serious criminal cases. Its intervention in political and administrative affairs as an executive organ of government gradually lessened as time passed and other political bodies were formed. First among these was the Council of Ten. The Magistracy was specifically an organ of judiciary power; this always remained its prerogative.

After Venice emerged as a political power, the amount of work to be dealt with caused damaging delay in the dispatching of cases. The Quarantia was divided in various periods into: the **Quarantia Civil Vecchia**, to handle cases from Venice itself and from the area ruled by the Doge; the **Quarantia Civil Nova**, which took care of civil suits involving citizens in provinces subject to the Republic; and the **Quarantia Criminal** which judged crimes in Venice itself and in the Doge's realm, excepting those which fell under the competence of the Council of Ten.

The hall was restored in its decors and furnishings in the XVII century. Of the original decoration there remains only a fragment of a fresco representing perhaps the upper part of St. Mark's Basilica with its great arch and foliated crowning.

Liagò

Hall of the Quarantia Civil Vecchia

Hall of the Armoury. Detail of Guariento's Fresco

THE HALL OF ARMAMENT OR OF GUARIENTO

This hall is named for the deposit of arms once stored here. Once it was connected by a staircase to the upper Hall of Arms of the Council of Ten. During the sessions, a number of arms were kept loaded and ready for use. Now the hall houses the old fresco by Guariento which was formerly in the Great Council Hall.

THE HALL OF THE GREAT COUNCIL

In 1141 there was already a «Consilium Sapentium» (Council of the Sages) working with the Doge as a political organ of the «Comune Veneciarium». The procedure for the election of its members at the outset is not very clear, but from the few data presently available it appears that there was a tendency to limit its membership to certain classes: the rich and the noble. At the same time, a concentration of power was kept from any single person. In 1286 a law was proposed by the Great Council itself providing for admission of only those members of the nobility whose paternal ancestors had served there before. This was approved only in 1297; it is the political stratagem known as **«The Barring of the Great Council».** It marks a decisive turn in the history of the Most Serene Republic. Each year the list of elegible men was compiled; there appeared the names of all those who had taken part in the Council in the past four years. An election was held, in which a candidate had to receive at least twelve votes to be admitted to the Council. Some members of families excluded at the start were later admitted through election. Later on, a system was perfected; the minimum age for admission was twenty-five.

Clearly the reform resulted for all practical purposes in the transformation of the Council into an hereditary assembly, accentuating its aristocratic character. Later this trend was reinforced by the institution of the **«Golden Book»** which existed to verify the noble origins of the Council members. Some revision of the exclusivist tendency took place eventually, not long after the «Barring». A concession was made to citizens who had acquired special merit during critical times, such as the period of the Baiamonte Tiepolo Conspiracy, or during the wars with Chioggia, Candia and the Turks. In the last years of the Republic, concessions were made to citizens who contributed large sums to the government.

Originally the Great Council exercised legislative and executive power; only after the «Barring» were many of its powers delegated to other governing units, first among them the Senate. However, the Council remained always the chief legislative power. It could grant pardons, ratify the election of the Doge, elect Senators and members of the courts, of the Council of Ten, the Doge's Councillors, the Grand Chancellor, the Avogadori, the Suppliers, the Censors, and so on. The Great Council grew gradually from *three hundred* to more than *one thousand six hundred members*. The Hall

Hall of the Great Council

which seated the highest Magistracy was located in various places in the Doges' Palace, as the Palace itself changed.

We have already mentioned the development of the Hall, built between 1340 and 1366. In fact the first commission issued for painted decors was given to **Guariento** of Padua, then a renowned artist, highly esteemed for works done mainly in Padua. He painted the great fresco «*The Coronation of the Virgin*» on the wall over the throne; work was completed about 1368. In spite of the fire, many sections of it remain, though in poor condition. The fresco was rediscovered in 1903 after having been forgotten, behind the huge canvas by Tintoretto. After removal, it was placed in the small adjacent hall.

The Signoria once again took an active interest toward 1382 in finishing the Great Council Hall, entrusting responsibility to the Procurators of St. Mark's. Perhaps Guariento had already done other paintings; in any case, from that time on, many artists worked in this colossal pictorial decoration. A first series of frescoes was gradually substituted in part by oil paintings on canvas, as the early works deteriorated because of humidity and the passing of time. The names of the artists may be found in documents of various periods.

Hall of the Great Council. Siege of Scutari by Paolo Veronese

Hall of the Great Council. The Apotheosis by Paolo Veronese ▶

Hall of the Great Council. The Venetian Fleet departing for the Battle against Barbarossa by Francesco Bassano

Very frequently, however, the extent of their work is not known. They are: **Antonio Veneziano, Gentile da Fabriano, Michelino da Besozzo, Pisanello, Alvise Vivarini (1499), Jacobello del Fiore, Gianbono.**

After this first period of intense work, there followed a long break owed above all to political events. This was the era of Doge **Francesco Foscari** and the conquest of the mainland, immediately followed by the reawakening of territorial ambitions and expansion of Ottoman power, which conquered Constantinople in 1453. Noteworthy were the battles waged by the Republic against Milan and, in 1508, the organization of the League of Cambrai which pitted Venice in a long struggle against Europe's strongest states.

For these reasons, the decoration of the Great Council Hall was resumed only after 1470. Unfinished areas were completed, and the areas of earlier work by then lost or damaged were renewed. But by this time taste also was changing; the pure Gothic expression was losing vitality while the new language of the Renaissance was taking hold. This is the period of **Gentile and Giovanni Bellini; Alvise Vivarini; Carpaccio; Titian, Pordenone, Tintoretto** and **Veronese.** Only the last two

Hall of the Great Council. Conquest of Constantinople by Jacopo Palma the Younger (Detail)

among these artists also worked on the redecoration of the hall after *the fire of 1577*.

On that occasion the fire was extinguished with the utmost difficulty, when it had almost reached the corner by the Ponte della Paglia. Some hours before, the blaze had broken out beneath the Hall of Scrutiny near the Porta della Carta. Walls and architectural elements of the windows suffered heavy damage, while the wooden warts of the roof and attics were completely destroyed, as were the paintings and frescoes and furnishings. The Signoria provided at once for the most urgent needs. The very stability of the edifice itself seemed so precarious that complete demolition and the construction of a new, different building was proposed. Numerous projects were presented, among them a design by **Palladio.** After animated discussions, the majority decided to restore the ruined areas and preserve the XIV—XV appearance of the building.

For this reason, then, the project of **Antonio Rusconi** was accepted. He proposed to restore the rooms making no changes save in the interior decoration.

After the fire the monk **Girolamo Bardi** was assigned the task of studying the themes for the paintings. Assisting him were two Stewards, **Jacopo Marcello** and **Jacopo Contarini.** Two important sujects from Venetian history were added to the usual theme of *the struggle between the Papacy and the Empire* with Venice as mediator and **Alexander III, Frederick Barbarossa** and **Sebastiano Ziani** as protagonists. These new themes were *the enterprises of the Fourth Crusade* and *the war of Chioggia.*

The ceiling, reflecting the tastes of the period, was conceived as a flat surface divided into large panels which were framed by gilded, carved cornices. Before, it had been an open-beam ceiling. Entrusted to **Cristoforo Sorte,** designer, the work was finished in 1582.

The first commission for paintings was given to **Tintoretto** and **Veronese** in 1579; shortly afterward **Jacopo Palma the Younger** and **Francesco Bassano** were also engaged. In 1584, the ceiling was virtually finished; many of the paintings had been placed by 1582.

For the walls more time was required. The work probably began around 1590, to be completed in the first years of the 1600's. The «*Paradise*» by **Tintoretto** merits an essay in itself. The artist, then very old, completed it between 1588 and 1594.

Hall of the Great Council. The Chioggia War by Paolo Veronese

The Chioggia War by Paolo Veronese (Detail)

Hall of the Great Council. Paradise by Jacopo Tintoretto
Paradise by Jacopo Tintoretto (Detail)

Paradise by Jacopo Tintoretto (Detail)

THE PAINTINGS OF THE PASSAGEWAY OF THE GREAT COUNCIL

The decoration of the Hall bears traces of a hurried and unsystematic scheme of restoration.

By **Jacopo Palma the Younger:** «*Concord*» (monochrome), «*Doge Marcantonio Memmo Before the Virgin*» and, last, «*Religion*» (monochrome). In the central painting, in addition to the figure of the Doge and of Ss. Mark, Anthony Abbot, Louis and Roch, are also symbolically represented the various city subjects of the Republic: Padua, Vicenza, Verona, Treviso, Brescia, Palmanova.

On the opposite wall, by **Domenico Tintoretto:** «*The People of the Sea Offer the Model of a Galley to St. Justine*», «*The Transfiguration of Christ*», «*Doge Giovanni Bembo Before Venice*». The canvases were painted about 1620. The painting «*Venice Kneeling Before the Virgin*» is by **Sebastiano Bombelli.**

THE PAINTINGS OF THE HALL OF THE QUARANTIA CIVIL VECCHIA

G. Battista Lorenzetti: «*Venice Receiving the Sceptre of Dominion*» (1630, circa); **Andrea Celesti:** «*Moses Orders the Calf of Gold Destroyed*» (about mid-XVII century). Both bear the arms and initials of Venetian magistrates who belonged to the Quarantia. Also by **Andrea Celesti:** «*The Slaughter of the Idolatrous Jews*». **Pietro Malombra:** «*The Annunciation*» (over the large arch of the window) and «*Venice Accepts Pleas from its Citizens*». This painting is clearly divided into two sections by a small capital already here years before the canvas was placed.

THE PAINTINGS OF THE HALL OF ARMAMENT OR OF GUARIENTO

Guariento: «*The Coronation of the Virgin*». The fresco was removed from its original location in 1903 and was placed in sections in this room. The parts remaining show the Redeemer in the act of crowning the Virgin prostrate at his feet, surrounded by angels and saints in stepped rows of stalls. Below are the Evangelists, as well as Patriarchs and Prophets of the Old Testament.

THE PAINTINGS OF THE GREAT COUNCIL HALL

Ceiling, central band:

Jacopo Tintoretto: «*Doge Nicolò da Ponte Receives a Laurel Crown from Venice*» (rectangular panel in centre). In the two ovals are, respectively, «*The Apotheosis of Venice*» by **Paolo Veronese** and «*Venice, Crowned by Victory, Welcomes Her Subject Provinces*» by **Jacopo Palma the Younger**.

Left lateral strip, beginning from entrance door, in rectangular panels with rounded angles, alternating with diversiform panels:

Paolo Veronese: «*The Siege of Scutari*». From 1453, year of the conquest of Constantinople, until 1481, year of the death of Mohammed II, Venice had to give up many overseas territories and sign treaties favourable to the Ottoman Empire, then in full military and economic development. The defense and liberation of Scutari, besieged by the Turks, took place in 1474, while Antonio Loredan was Steward.

Francesco Bassano: «*Venetian Victory over the Ferrarese at Polesella*». After a mutual agreement was reached by Pope Sixtus IV and the Genoese and Sienese states, Venice began in 1482 a victorious campaign against Ercole I, Duke of Ferrara.

Jacopo Tintoretto: «*Venetian Victory over the Ferrarese at Argenta*». This, another triumph in the war against Ercole I, took place also in 1482.

Jacopo Tintoretto: «*The Venetians Conquer Gallipoli*». The war which Venice waged to win Ferrara was extended into other regions. In 1484, the Venetian fleet won the important port of Gallipoli. After the treaty was signed, it was restored to Ferdinand in exchange for other territories.

Francesco Bassano: «*The Venetians Defeat the Troops of the Emperor Maximilian in the Cadore*». In 1508, the Emperor of Austria invaded the territories of Venice, but he was defeated by the Venetian armies in the Cadore. Shortly afterward, the League of Cambrai rose against the Republic.

Jacopo Palma the Younger: «*The Conquest of Padua*». After the critical period following the institution of the League of Cambrai, the Most Serene Republic tried to re-conquer its mainland territories. Padua was re-taken in 1509.

Right lateral strip. **Paolo Veronese:** *«The Conquest of Smyrna».* The city fell into the hands of the Venetians in 1471. The episode is merely one of many in a long, vicissitudinous war against the Turks and Mohammed II.

Francesco Bassano: *«Victory of the Venetians over the Milanese at Casalmaggiore».* With the conquest of the mainland, which was begun during the reign of Doge Francesco Foscari, Venice launched a long and taxing struggle against the Duchy of Milan. It was an uninterrupted series of battles, alliances and treaties which lasted until the death of Duke Filippo Maria Visconti in 1447. The victory of Casalmaggiore in 1446 allowed the Republic to retain its territories as far as the River Adda.

Jacopo Tintoretto: *«The Venetians Conquer Riva on Lake Garda».* Stefano Contarini, having defeated Visconti's fleet on Lake Garda, set sail at once for Riva, taking the city. The land army simultaneously occupied Lonato and Salò.

Jacopo Tintoretto: *«The Defense of Brescia».* In 1436, Venice and Milan reopened hostilities. Brescia was besieged two years later, but the garrison, headed by Francesco Barbaro, took decisive action against Piccinino, Milanese commander, who was forced to abandon the enterprise.

Francesco Bassano: *«Victory of the Venetians over the Milanese at Maclodio».* This episode took place in 1428, when Carmagnola overcame Milanese troops, which suffered a severe loss of men and material. The peace which followed immediately afterward reconfirmed Venetian dominion over the territories of Brescia, to which were added those of Bergamo and Cremona.

Jacopo Palma the Younger: *«Victory of the Venetians Over the Milanese on the Po, near Cremona».* The naval battle took place in 1427 near Casalmaggiore. Notwithstanding the victory, Francesco Bembo could not overcome Cremona afterwards.

In other panels are monochromatic canvases by various painters: **Leonardo Corona, l'Aliense, Pietro Longo, Francesco Montemezzano, il Vicentino** and **Palma the Younger.**

The frieze is made up of a series of canvases with portraits of the first 76 doges. The assignment was given to **Jacopo** Tintoretto, only to be realized finally by **Domenico,** his son.

On the walls are illustrated to the right, **THE STRUGGLE BETWEEN THE EMPEROR FREDERICK BARBAROSSA AND THE POPE ALEXANDER III AND THE MEDIATION OF DOGE SEBASTIANO ZIANI (1172—1178).**

The series is made up of twelve canvases:

Benedetto and Carlo Caliari: *«The Encounter in Venice Between Pope Alexander III and Doge Sebastiano Ziani Before the School of Charity».*

Benedetto and Carlo Caliari: *«Pope Alexander III and Doge Sebastiano Ziani Send Ambassadors to Barbarossa to Make Peace».* Both canvases are signed.

Leandro Bassano: *«Pope Alexander III Offers the Blessed Candle to Doge Ziani».*

Jacopo Tintoretto: *«The Ambassadors Sent by Doge Ziani Ask Barbarossa in Vain to Grant Peace for the Pope's Sake».*

Francesco Bassano: *«The Venetian Fleet Prepares to Leave the Quai at St. Mark's Against Barbarossa».*

Paolo dei Franceschi, il Fiammingo: *«Alexander III Blessed Doge Ziani Who Prepares to Leave with the Fleet».*

Domenico Tintoretto: *«The Battle of Salvore».*

Andrea Vicentino: *«Doge Ziani, Returning Victorious from the Battle, Received the Blessed Ring from the Pope».*

Jacopo Palma the Younger: *«Pope Alexander III and Doge Ziani Send Young Otto to Barbarossa to Propose Peace».* Otto, son of Frederick, had been taken during the Battle of Salvore».

Federico Zuccari: *«Emperor Frederick, Arriving in Venice, Pays Public Homage to Pope Alexander III».*

Girolamo Gamberato: *«Pope Alexander III, Emperor Frederick Barbarossa and Doge Sebastiano Ziani Reach Ancona».*

Giulio d'Angelo del Moro: *«Doge Ziani in the Roman Church of St. John Lateran Receives Gifts from the Pope».*

On the left, **THE FOURTH CRUSADE AND THE CONQUEST OF CONSTANTINOPLE (1202—1205).**

Carlo Saraceni and **Giovanni Leclerc:** *«Doge Enrico Dandolo and the Crusader Captains in St. Mark's Swear*

Theyr Loyalty to the Pacts Before Beginning the Undertaking». Leclerc completed the work, left unfinished at the death of Saraceni.

Andrea Vicentino: «*The Crusaders Conquer the City of Zara*».

Domenico Tintoretto: «*The Taking of Zara*».

Domenico Tintoretto: «*The First Surrender of Constantinople*» (1203).

Andrea Vicentino: *Young Alexius Asks Help from Doge Enrico Dandolo*».

Jacopo Palma the Younger: «*The Crusader Army Assaults Constantinople and Conquers it for the Second Time*« (1204).

Andrea Vicentino: «*Baldwin of Flanders Is Elected Emperor of the East by Doge Dandolo and the Crusader Princes in Constantinople*».

Antonio Aliense: «*Coronation of Baldwin as Emperor of the East*».

On the end wall facing the throne: **THE CHIOGGIA WAR:**

Paolo Veronese: «*The Return of Doge Andrea Contarini to Venice Following the Venetian Victory over the Genoese at Chioggia*». The event took place in 1380 when the Genoese fleet, besieged near Chioggia, finally accepted unconditional surrender. For Venice, this was a great victory after being threatened with invasion. The very existence of the Republic was at stake. For the first time, Venice had been attacked and was forced to resist in the very waters of its own lagoon. Its wisdom in military matters and the utter abnegation of the population made it possible to turn back the Genoese. The fortunes of Venice had been eroded in the long war which pitted the two great maritime republics against each other; both were utterly dedicated to the struggle. Genoa, torn by internal strife, was forced to give way before the stronger and more united adversary.

Above the windows: canvases of allegorical subjects by **Marco Vecellio** and **Aliense.**

On the wall above the dais is **Tintoretto's** grandiose painting «*Paradise*», accomplished by the master in his late years, immediately before his death in 1594. He was helped by his son **Domenico** and by **Jacopo Palma the Younger** as well as by many pupils from his studio.

Hall of the Quarantia Civil Nova

THE HALL OF THE QUARANTIA CIVIL NOVA

Mention has already been made of the formation, the duties and the matters handled by this Magistracy, in the section concerning the Quarantia Civil Vecchia. It is worth bearing in mind that it was instituted in 1492 and that it had responsibility for hearing civil cases involving citizens of the provinces subject to Venice.

This hall was also damaged in the fire of 1577. It was completely restored in a short time, assuming its present aspect. The ceiling with its gilded beams dates from that restoration. Later, though, the original furnishings were lost. The present seats are imitations of the older ones. The large window corresponds with the third window from the right on the façade toward the Piazzetta. Above and below the Quarantia were located other rooms which in former periods were used as offices of secretaries and scribes.

Filippo Zaniberti: «*Justice Discovers Truth Hidden by Vices*». **Antonio del Foler:** «*Venice Entrusts the Resolution of Disputes to Justice*». **G. Battista Lorenzetti:** «*Venice Receives the Doge's Cap in the Presence of Neptune*».

Hall of the Scrutiny

THE HALL OF SCRUTINY

As mentioned before, this wing of the Doges' Palace was built between 1424 and 1440, during the reign of **Francesco Foscari**. It was intended to resemble the wing built nearly a century before on the quayside, thus maintaining a single, unified architectural concept in the whole.

In the loggias were placed neither stairways not rooms for conferences and meetings. Thus the feeling of an open, spacious structure was accentuated. In the closed upper portion a second great hall was located. This was the Hall of Scrutiny because of its function. At first it also housed the Public Library, an enormously rich collection of precious ancient volumes, the most important core of which was donated by Petrarch and Cardinal Bessarion. When the ·Republic decided to build the Marciana Library, giving the commission to Sansovino, this hall was completely freed of this secondary function. It continued to be used only for balloting; here Venetian patricians gathered to elect the new Doge or nominate members of other Magistracies. This was the site of secret voting, a part of the complicated system invented by the Most Serene Republic to avoid all intrigues, plots and subterfuges.

As far back as 1172, the election of the Doge was entrusted to eleven electors chosen in the Great Council. The «Concio Generalis» simply approved the nominations. In 1178 the electoral system became more complex: four electors named the forty who elected the Doge. Later, the forty became forty-one, to avoid the possibility of a tie vote. In 1268 a procedure was set up which, excepting for minor changes, was to last until the end of the Republic.

It is worthwhile describing this complex system to give the reader an idea of the precautions taken to prevent any upsetting of institutions and any personal transgressions. In the Great Council Hall gathered all patricians who had passed their thirtieth birthday. They made up the electoral body. The first move consisted of the extraction of one ballot from the urn by each man present. Only thirty ballots bore the word «Lector» and only thirty patricians who had drawn them were allowed to remain. These men, following the same procedure, were then reduced to nine. The nine, in secret ballot, elected forty delegates (each one of these, however, had to have received more than seven votes). The forty were then reduced to twelve, by drawing

Hall of the Scrutiny. Ceiling

Hall of the Scrutiny. Last Judgement by Jacopo Palma the Younger (Detail)

lots. The twelve in secret ballot elected twenty-five men. The twenty-five, once again using a system of drawing lots, were reduced to nine. The nine, in secret ballot, elected forty-five men. The forty-five, by drawing lots from the urn, were reduced to eleven, who finally elected (again in secret voting) the forty-one electors of the Doge. These, however, had to be confirmed by the Great Council; and this was not always done. Only after they had received that approval could the forty-one men go ahead with the regular conclave to elect the Doge. Each of the electors made his nomination by secret vote and after drawing lots, the electors decided which of the proposed names should be discussed and voted on first. The candidate who had obtained at least twenty-five votes was elected.

The key: b - balloting; sv - secret vote.

General Assembly: b, *thirty;* b, *nine;* sv, *forty;* b, *twelve;* sv, *twenty-five;* b, *nine;* sv, *forty-five;* b, *eleven;* sv, *forty-one electors to select the Doge;* sv, *election of the Doge, with at least twenty-five votes required.*

Hall of the Scrutiny. Conquest of Zara by Jacopo Tintoretto (Detail)

As we have already seen, the hall was also used as a Library; in 1531 **Sansovino,** in addition to the plan for its decoration, proposed to divide the hall into two sections to make it usable for both purposes.

Toward 1530 the pictorial decoration was begun; work went on for twelve years. The coffered ceiling was probably finished by about 1537, or in the following year at the latest. The canvases for the coffers had been painted by **Pordenone,** who was also the artist of the frieze. The subjects were chosen to depict *The Virtues.*

Later, the Most Serene Republic decided to sell the frieze and to substitute for it the *Portraits of the Doges,* giving the commission to **Titian,** who painted some of them. **Tintoretto,** too, collaborated on the work. In fact, he painted a famous *Battle of Lepanto,* a theme later used by **Il Vicentino.** In 1577 the hall was completely destroyed by fire. Supervision of its restoration was delegated to **Antonio da Ponte,** who began the work about 1582. Toward the end of the century, the operations was considered virtually complete. In 1599, work-

Hall of the Scrutiny. Battle of Lepanto by Andrea Vicentino ▶

leading to the loggia below was constructed the splendid *Triumphal Arch* raised in honor of **Francesco Morosini**, known as «the Peloponnesiac», immediately after his death in 1694. This monument was designed by the architect **Antonio Gaspari** and ornamented with paintings by **Gregorio Lazzarini**. The themes refer in allegory to the achievements of the great Venetian warrior and leader. He succeeded in winning important naval engagements and land wars, renewing for years the memory of past battles and conquests. Venice, whose prestige had been shaken for some time by the Turkish Empire, to which its overseas territories had been ceded little by little, now suddenly sprung up again. The reconquest of the Morea and of other territories was hailed in Venice with great enthusiasm, and the man responsible for these victories became the saviour of his country.

Hall of the Scrutiny. Triumphal Arch in honour of Francesco Morosini

THE PAINTINGS OF THE HALL OF SCRUTINY

Central area of the ceiling, oval panels:

Francesco Bassano: «*The Venetians Conquer Padua*». The episode took place in 1405 during the war which the Republic waged against the Carraresi, lords of Padua.

Camillo Ballini: «*The Victory of the Venetians over the Genoese at Trapani*». Genoa, allied with the Emperor Palaeologus in the conquest of the eastern throne, profited from the situation by occupying Galata and destroying the Venetian quarter of Constantinople. In the war which followed the encounter took place in 1265.

Andrea Vicentino: «*Venetian Naval Victory over the Pisans at Rhodes*». Unclear is the motive for this encounter between the two fleets sent out to the Holy Land in 1098 to take part in the Crusade ordered by Pope Urban II.

Giulio d'Angelo del Moro: «*The Venetians Conquer Jaffa*». Greatly threatened by Genoa's military and diplomatic action in the east, Venice won important ports on the Black Sea; in 1294 with the reconquest of Jaffa, they were again in control of the situation.

Francesco Montemezzano: «*The Conquest of Acre*». Before the opening of hostilities, both Republics, Genoa and Venice, had quarters in the city of Acre. After the naval battle in 1258, shown in this painting, the Most Serene Republic was sole ruler of Acre.

In other panels, episodes from Venetian history; monochromes and allegorical figures. By **Giulio d'Angelo del Moro:** «*Doge Domenico Michiel Refuses the Crown of Sicily*» and «*Doge Domenico Michiel Refuses the Crown of the East*».

By **Antonio Aliense:** «*Pietro Ziani Renounces the Title of Doge to Become a Monk*», and «*Doge Ordelafo Falier Dies Near the Walls of Zara*».

In the other diversiform panels: By **Camillo Ballini:** «*Faith*», «*Prudence*», «*Temperance*» and «*Public Trust*». By **Marco Vecellio:** «*Fortitude*», «*Justice*». By **Antonio Aliense:** «*Magnificence*», «*Harmony*», «*Naval Discipline*», «*Army Discipline*», «*Clemency*», «*Liberality*». By **Giulio Licinio:** «*Chance*», «*Fame*», «*Security*», «*Justice*», «*Victory*», «*Law*», «*Abundance*», «*Firmness*», «*Silence*», «*Vigilance*», «*Truth*».

On the tribune wall: **Andrea Vicentino** painted a frieze with figures of *Prophets* and *Evangelists*. Below, **Jacopo Palma the Younger** was commissioned to paint the large canvas depicting the «*Last Judgment*».

Continuing, **Jacopo Tintoretto:** «*Victory of the Vene-*

tians Against the Hungarians, and the Conquest of Zara». The city, sought by King Louis of Hungary, who wanted control of the region and an outlet to the sea, rebelled against Venetian power in 1347.

Andrea Vicentino: *«The Conquest of Cattaro».* This took place in 1379 during the war between Venice and Genoa, which would be concluded one year later in the lagoon near Chioggia.

Andrea Vicentino: *«The Battle of Lepanto».* This historic encounter took place in 1571 between the Turkish fleet of Ali Pasha and that of the allies under Don John of Austria. Among these allies were Venice, Spain, Tuscany, Savoy, Pope Pius V and others.

Pietro Bellotto: *«Victory of the Venetians over the Turks in Albania, and the Demolition of the Fortress of Margarita».* Shortly after the Battle of Lepanto, Francesco Corner, in the continuing struggle against the Turks, conquered this heavily fortified castle in Albania.

Pietro Liberi: *«Victory of the Venetians over the Turks in the Dardanelles».* In 1645, as hostilities were resumed against the Ottoman Empire, the Venetian fleet blockaded the Dardanelles. Many encounters were won by Venice, but with the passing of time, the Turks inexorably won back their territory in the archipelago; in 1669, with the conquest of Candia, they definitively excluded Venice from commerce with the east.

Andrea Vicentino: *«The Venetians Prepare Their Defense of the Lagoon Against Invasion by King Pippin».* A now legendary event of the early history of Venice, dating from 810. Pippin's fleet was destroyed in the lagoon when the Venetians succeeded in luring the heavy French boats to run aground.

Andrea Vicentino: *«Pippin's Army on a Boat Bridge Attempts to Reach the City of Venice and Take It by Surprise».*

Sante Peranda: *«Venetian Naval Victory at Jaffa».* Doge Domenico Michiel, in 1123, came to the aid of the King of Jerusalem, Baldwin II, met the Egyptian fleet off the port of Jaffa and defeated it.

Antonio Aliense: *«The Conquest of Tyre».* The event was part of the successful campaign of the Venetian fleet in Syria, under the command of Doge Domenico Michiel.

Marco Vecellio: *«Victory of the Venetians at Cape Matapan».* This encounter took place off Cape Matapan in 1149, between the fleets of Roger II and Venice.

Over the windows, *allegorical figures* by **Sebastiano Ricci, Antonio Aliense** and **Marco Vecellio.**

THE HALL OF THE QUARANTIA CRIMINAL

The hall was the seat of an important magistracy whose functions have already been discussed in the section on the Quarantia Civil Vecchia. It is worthwhile remembering that the Quarantia Criminal took part in the Senate assemblies after the XIV century. The members of the magistracy in private assembly nominated the three «Presidenti sopra Uffici» or higher powers, to discipline all the civil ministeries.

The furnishing of the hall and the pictorial decorations were completely lost after the fall of the Republic. A painting by Gabriele Bella, XVIII century, shows this hall during a sitting. This work is now in the Querini-Stampalia Foundation. On the basis of it, a recent restoration was made possible. Above the tribunal there is a single precious *gilded leather*, the only one still in the Palace. In its centre, amid floral decorations, are the arms of three noble Venetian families, painted at a later date. The ceiling is original; it has

Hall of the Quarantia Criminal. Lion Passant by Jacobello del Fiore

painted, gilded beams. Along the frieze is a series of coats-of-arms.

There follow two other halls stripped of the original decor, save for fireplaces dating from the first years of the XVI century. These two halls are now known as the **Magistracy for Criminal Procedures** and **Magistracy of Laws.**

In the first are the original statues of *Adam* and *Eve* by **Antonio Rizzo,** once on the façade of the Foscari Arch.

THE PAINTINGS OF THE HALL OF THE QUARANTIA CRIMINAL

Jacobello del Fiore: «*Lion Passant*». (This painting was located in the offices of the Magistracy which ruled on blasphemy cases, in the Palace of the Camerlenghi); **Antonio Balestra:** «*Doge Giovanni Corner Kneeling Before the Virgin*».

THE NEW PRISONS

The area originally intended to serve for prison cells in the Palace had never really been adequate to the need. Neither were the various attempts to solve the problem truly satisfactory. Thus during the XVI century, the Council of Ten was forced to consider some location outside of the Palace. The most convenient place was in the area facing the canal near the Ponte della Paglia. At first it was thought that some use might be made of the old houses then on that site, but this idea was abandoned. The structures were pulled down and a special building was constructed. By 1566 this first building must have been completed. It corresponds to the section of the structure farthest from the quayside, to the left of the Bridge of Sighs, which connects it to the Doges' Palace. It is evident from the plan that this is the oldest part of these New Prisons, as it is very similar to the plan of «The Wells» and because it is quite independent in its arrangement of storeys and stairs from the rest of the fabric. It is a fact that although the government clearly hoped to better the prisoners' conditions by building a new structure, this was no better than the older prison. This is the area now open to the public, though limited to one floor only. A corridor used for patrolling runs along three sides of the cell block while the transverse corridor inside divides the cells into two double rows. They are small and dark.

The New Prisons were enlarged according to a program carried out over successive periods.

It is quite certain that this expansion began at the canal as an extension of the original building; it developed gradually toward the Basin of St. Mark and the Calle degli Albanesi. In 1574 part of the prisoners in the Palace were transferred here.

In 1580, the Council of Ten voted again to confine all prisoners outside the Palace. The construction of a single, large Prison was by then necessary. After this period no further delays held up the progress of the work. Logically the area chosen was between the quayside and St. Apollonia, in continuation of the one already used for this purpose.

Antonio da Ponte and **Zamaria de' Piombi** were commissioned separately to submit their plans for the project. These were quite similar, however, in their ground plans. **Da Ponte,** who was eventually given the commission for the work, submitted a plan for a building around a central courtyard, connecting the buildings

Prisons. Façade toward the Quay

New Prisons. Entrance to the Bridge of Sighs

already standing. The description of the structure facing the quayside toward the Island of San Giorgio, more or less corresponds to the structure built later and still standing today. This is true of the general architectonic form and of the use. The hall on the first floor on the quayside of the building was for the Magistracy of the «*Signori di Notte al Criminal*».

On the death of Da Ponte in 1597, **Antonio Contin** was made Superintendent of Works in the Palace. He went ahead with the plans of Da Ponte.

Little by little, as the Prisons were gradually completed, larger numbers of prisoners were moved into the building. The first to be transferred here the feeble and the ill, who were lodged in the «Moceniga Prison», a hospital, or in larger and better lighted cells. The elimination of the greater part of the prisons in the Doges' Palace logically brought to a close the work of enlarging the New Prisons. These were virtually completed by 1610.

The ground plan and the arangement of the cells and corridors was a marked improvement over the old situation, although it was still bound to the traditional concept of prison architecture. Not only did the areas have larger dimensions and greater height, but even the actual illumination of cells, though still indirect, was better. Because the Prisons were built over a number of years and many designers and supervisors were involved, the ground plan now seems confusing in some areas. There were also later changes made. The outside of the building, on the other hand, has a remarkable unity of architectural style, where variations reflect only a different function of the interior. Toward the quayside, the structure designed by Da Ponte shows great coherence in its arrangement as well as a clear differentiation in the uses of various areas. It was well built according to the dictates of late XVI century style. Nowhere on the outside of the building is there the slightest hint of the use to which the place was actually put. The ground floor and huge windows of the main floor break up the strong wall of squared Istrian stone blocks, making it seem less severe. Not so on the façade which faces Rio della Canonica, nor on those toward Calle degli Albanesi and the inner courtyard.

The whole of this structure is built with Istrian stone blocks, and it represents one of the earliest examples in Europe of a single-unit block construction used as a state prison.

Antonio Contin was the designer of the BRIDGE OF SIGHS.

At the end of the century the Republic decided to connect the Doges' Palace directly with the New Prisons at the point where the cells for prisoners of the Council of Ten were located. This was the oldest part of the structure, clearly defined at that time even in its external architectural design. The bridge was begun in the first months of 1600 and completed before 1602. It is apparent that it was inserted into the fabric after the façade was completed. The ashlars and especially the ornamental motif of the keystone at the centre of the window architrave appear on the interior, as does the shape of the crowning, over the entrances, although altered and even partly eliminated by the structural elements of the bridge itself.

The construction of this enclosed and covered stone bridge displays Contin's baroque taste, yet the bridge itself answered a real practical need. It facilitated internal communications the special nature of which demanded that these routes be autonomous and independent of each other, yet within the structure. Taken as a whole, the bridge is remarkably original in concept and execution. As one leaves the Prisons, he finds that the bridge has two separate corridors with a wall running between them, both reaching the full length of the bridge. The corridor on the right leads to the first main floor of the Palace, into the halls of the Magistracy of Laws and of the Quarantia Criminal. The left-hand passageway goes to the halls of the Avogaria and of the Prisoners' Parlour. Both corridors are also connected to the service stairway which runs from «The Wells» below to «The Leads» above.

«*Leads*» is the name given to some cells beneath the Palace roof. One may assume that these were already in existence in the second half of the XV century. They became famous because **Casanova** was imprisoned here before his daring escape, which he tells of in his Memoirs. Today very little remains of this part of the building.

On the same floor, following the narrow passage there is the *Torture Chamber*, also knows as the «Court of the Room of the Cord», as can be deduced from a description in a document of 1588. This room is included in the tour of that area of the Palace which also includes the *Secret Chancery, the Offices of the Grand Chancellor, the Secretary of Nominations* and *the Ducal Notary*. In this area all the flights of the service stairs meet, making a vertical passageway through the Palace.

Ducal Palace. The Leads and the Torture Chamber

THE HALL OF THE CENSORS

Here sat the magistracy instituted in 1517, explicitly to see that laws providing for honest elections were obeyed. Two men elected from the Great Council prevented conspiracies on the part of those who wanted to seize power.

In 1509 **Pietro Lombardo** began to restore it; afterwards other changes were made, and work was completed in 1549, when **Scarpagnino** died.

The room was redecorated after the fall of the Republic. Its ceiling is original, as is the frieze with crests of the 266 censors who were in power from 1517.

THE HALL OF NOTARIES OR OF THE AVOGARIA

The first information we have about this magistracy dates from the XII century. Its function was that of public prosecutor in councils. The Avogadori kept watch over the observance of the statutes and the payment of fines or penalties. At least one of the Avogadori attended sittings of the Great Council and Senate. He held veto power when decisions ran contrary to laws. He also was present at the sittings of the Council of Ten. There were three of these magistrates; their tenure lasted one year. The great wall clock marks only six hours. From here one may pass through one of the two doors on the left into the prisons of the Palace called «The Wells» or through the other onto the loggia.

155

Hall of the Avogaria

Hall of the Avogaria. The Holy Spirit and Portraits of two Avogadori by
Sebastiano Bombelli

THE HALL OF THE COFFER

Among other duties the Avogadori were required to keep up to date the books listing the various honourary orders to which the families belonged. To compile these records and keep them current, hearings were held to confirm the rank of nobility and to recognize the citizens. Records were kept in two books in this room: The Golden Book, listing noble families; and the Silver Book, with the names of citizens' families.

Of the old fittings of the room there remains only a precious wall armoire with gilt decorations.

THE HALL OF THE MARITIME SUPERINTENDENT OF SUPPLIES

When a powerful fleet was built in 1571, the Republic instituted an assembly of four senators and others chosen from the Great Council, each of whom had a specific technical competence. These men organized and managed this huge enterprise, down to the smallest detail. Later they were given duties which went from arming warships, to recruiting seamen to the victualing of crews and everything concerning the needs of the fleets.

The furnishings date from the XVIII century.

Hall of the Scrigno

OFFICE OF THE SECRETARY OF NOMINATIONS

In this little room worked the functionary required to keep registers of all proposals made, all elections, and the respective expiration dates of all Government appointments, both regular and special.

OFFICE OF THE DOGE'S SEAL

This office was a dependency of the Chancery. The official, or «Bollador», had responsibility for affixing the Doge's seal, giving the «nulla obtat» or sanction for all projects. He also was responsible for keeping records of acts of clemency and amnesty, as accorded by the Great Council.

THE DUCAL CHANCERY

This hall has lost its former fittings. It was the office of the Grand Chancellor and his staff. He was the foremost spokesman for the original citizens, who were not part of the nobility but enjoyed noblemen's rights. His election was the duty of the Great Council, and his appointment, like the Doge's, was for life. His functions were directing the Chanceries (Ducal and Secret) who kept the archives of elections, as well as the texts of international treaties concluded by the Most Serene Republic.

Hall of the Milizia da Mar. The Queen of Sheba before Solomon (Detail)

THE PAINTINGS OF THE HALL OF THE CENSORS

On the walls from right to left:

Domenico Tintoretto: «*Annunciation and Portraits of Three Avogadori*». **Domenico Tintoretto**: «*Christ the Redeemer and Portraits of Ten Censors*». **Domenico Tintoretto**: «*Madonna and Child with Nine Censors*». **Domenico Tintoretto**: «*Portraits of Four Censors*». **Domenico Tintoretto**: «*Portraits of Five Censors*». At the centre of this painting is a small capital with a panel depicting the «*Madonna and Child*» on a gold background from the **Studio of Vivarini**. **Domenico Tintoretto**: «*Portraits of Five Censors*». **Pietro Malombra**: «*Deposition of Christ and Portraits of Four Censors*». **Domenico Tintoretto**: «*The Holy Spirit and Portraits of Ten Censors*». **Domenico Tintoretto**: «*Coronation of the Virgin and Portraits of Eight Censors*». None of these is of great value; and they are more likely the work of pupils of Domenico Tintoretto than by the master himself. They date from the first two decades of the XVII century.

THE PAINTINGS OF THE HALL OF THE NOTARIES

On the walls, beginning at the entrance:

Leandro Bassano: «*The Virgin in Glory and Portraits of Three Avogadori*». **Domenico Tintoretto**: «*The Dead Christ and Portraits of Three Avogadori*». **Domenico Tintoretto**: «*St. Mark in Glory and Portraits of Three Avogadori and Two Notaries*».

On the wall where the clock is placed:

Tiberio Tinelli: «*The Virgin in Glory and Portraits of Six Avogadori*». **Sebastiano Bombelli**: «*The Holy Spirit and Portraits of Two Avogadori*». **Domenico Tintoretto**: «*Ss. Anthony Abbot, Peter the Apostle, Jerome and Portraits of Three Avogadori*».

On the wall facing the entrance: **Pietro Uberti**: *Portraits of Three Avogadori*». **Domenico Tintoretto**: «*Portraits of Three Avogadori and Three Notaries*».

On the window wall: **Domenico Tintoretto**: «*Christ, the Virtues and Portraits of Three Avogadori and a Notary*». **Domenico Tintoretto**: «*Portraits of Two Notaries*».

THE PAINTINGS OF THE HALL OF THE COFFER

Anonymous: «*Portrait of Three Avogadori*». **In the style of Uberti**: «*Portrait of Three Avogadori*». **Pietro Uberti**: «*Portrait of Three Avogadori*». **In the style of Uberti**: «*Virgin and Child with Portraits of Three Avogadori*». **Vincenzo Guarana**: «*Portrait of Three Avogadori*». **Tiberio Tinelli**: «*The Virgin in Glory and Portraits of Six*

Avogadori». **Nicolò Renieri:** *«The Virgin in Glory and Child and Portraits of Three Avogadori»*. **Anonymous:** *«Portrait of an Avogadore»*. **Pietro Uberti:** *«Portrait of Three Avogadori»*. **In the style of Uberti:** *«Portrait of Three Avogadori»*. **Alessandro Longhi:** *«Portrait of a Notary»*. **Alessandro Longhi:** *«Portrait of Three Avogadori»*. **Alessandro Longhi:** *«Portrait of a Notary»*.

THE PAINTINGS OF THE HALL OF THE MARITIME SUPERINTENDENT
Anonymous, in the style of Tiepolo: *«Adoration of the Magi»*. **Anonymous (perhaps from Ricci studio):** *«The Descent of the Holy Spirit»*. **Anonymous, in the style of Tiepolo:** *«The Queen of Sheba Before Solomon»*. **Anonymous:** *St. Mark the Evangelist»*.

THE PAINTINGS OF THE OFFICE OF THE SECRETARY OF NOMINATIONS
Donato Veneziano: *«Lion Passant»* (1459). **Domenico Tintoretto:** *«Resurrection of Christ»* (fragment).

THE PAINTINGS OF THE ROOM OF THE DOGE'S SEAL
Filippo Zaniberti: *«Doge Giovanni Corner at the Island of San Giorgio»*. **Sebastiano Bombelli:** *«Portrait of Three Avogadori»*. **Nicolò Renieri:** *«Portrait of Two Notaries»*. **Nicolò Cassana:** *«Portrait of a Notary»*. **Nicolò Cassana:** *«Portrait of Two Notaries»*. **Sebastiano Bombelli:** *«Portrait of Three Avogadori»*. **Sebastiano Bombelli:** *«Portrait of Two Avogadori»*. **Anonymous:** *«Portrait of Three Avogadori»*.

THE PAINTINGS OF THE HALL OF THE DOGES' CHANCERY
Camillo Ballini: *«Frieze with Cherubs and Figures Bearing the Signs of the Zodiac»*.

THE WELLS

In January, 1531 the Republic decided to restore the wing of the Palace next to the canal. This included various chambers: the Halls of the Pregadi, of the Council of Ten, of the Quarantia Criminal, and of the Avogaria. The estimates for the work also included plans for a new prison, destined only for those convicted by the Council of Ten. Its cells were planned and built on the ground floor of the Palace of Justice, far from and quite separate from the prisons then in the Palace itself. They were directly connected by a service stair to the Hall of the Three Chiefs of the Council, on the upper floor. In a roughly square area, bounded by the two entrance halls from the canal side and by the portico of the courtyard and by the canal itself, nineteen cells were located.

The Wells. The Interior of a Cell

These were called «The Wells» for the impression conjured up by the narrowness of the cells, the humid wells and the lack of ventilation. The ground plan is common to prisons of that period: a corridor running around the external side of the cells, which are grouped in a double block in the centre. The doors and vents open only onto the corridor. Every cell was numbered on the stone architrave over the door with a Roman numeral carved upside down, in a seeming attempt to impede a full understanding of the prison's ground-plan. The structure itself is entirely built of huge blocks of Istrian stone. One cell is still furnished with original fittings, including the wooden facing of the walls, the ceiling, the pavement and the plank-bed, raised on stone blocks. A small shelf and a bucket completed the furnishings.

THE MUSEUM OF THE PALACE

The Museum has been located for the past few years in the rooms on the ground floor facing the Piazzetta and the Basin of St. Mark. These were once used as stables and prison cells. The Museum includes all the original pieces of sculpture which were removed from the façade during the structural restoration of 1875—1887. There are many columns and capitals from the external portico and from the fourteenth century loggia. These are partly damaged. Also here are the original capitals of the Sansovino Loggetta, and so on. In one of these rooms there still exists a column which remains from Ziani's ancient structure.

Sculpture Museum. Room One

INDEX OF NAMES AND PLACES

165

LIST OF THE DOGES AND YEAR OF THEIR ELECTION

Paolo Lucio Anafesto	697
Marcello Tegelliano	717
Orso Ipato	726
Teodato Ipato	742
Galla Gaulo	755
Domenico Monegario	756
Maurizio Galbaio	764
Giovanni Galbaio	787
Obelerio Antenereo	804

The seat of Government transferred from Malamocco to Rivoalto.

Angelo Partecipazio	811
Giustiniano Partecipazio	827
Giovanni I Partecipazio	829
Pietro Tradonico	836
Orso Partecipazio	864
Giovanni II Partecipazio	881
Pietro Candiano	887
Pietro Tribuno	888
Orso II Partecipazio	912
Pietro II Candiano	932
Pietro Partecipazio	939
Pietro III Candiano	942
Pietro IV Candiano	959
Pietro I Orseolo	976
Vitale Candiano	978
Tribuno Memmo	979
Pietro Orseolo	991
Ottone Orseolo	1008
Pietro Centranico	1026
Domenico Flabanico	1032
Domenico Contarini	1043
Domenico Selvo	1071
Vitale Falier	1084
Vitale I Michiel	1096
Ordelafo Falier	1102
Domenico Michiel	1118
Pietro Polani	1130
Domenico Morosini	1148
Vitale II Michiel	1156
Sebastiano Ziani	1172
Orio Malipiero	1178
Enrico Dandolo	1192
Pietro Ziani	1205
Jacopo Tiepolo	1229
Marino Morosini	1249
Reniero Zeno	1253
Lorenzo Tiepolo	1268
Jacopo Contarini	1275
Giovanni Dandolo	1280
Pietro Gradenigo	1298
Marino Zorzi	1311
Giovanni Soranzo	1312
Francesco Dandolo	1329
Bartolomeo Gradenigo	1339
Andrea Dandolo	1343
Marino Faliero	1354
Giovanni Gradenigo	1355
Giovanni Dolfin	1356
Lorenzo Celsi	1361
Marco Corner	1365
Andrea Contarini	1368
Michele Morosini	1382
Antonio Venier	1382
Tommaso Mocenigo	1414
Francesco Foscari	1423
Pasquale Malipiero	1457
Cristoforo Moro	1462
Nicolò Tron	1471
Nicolò Marcello	1473
Pietro Mocenigo	1474
Andrea Vendramin	1476
Giovanni Mocenigo	1478
Marco Barbarigo	1485
Agostino Barbarigo	1486
Leonardo Loredan	1501
Antonio Grimani	1521
Andrea Gritti	1523
Pietro Lando	1539
Francesco Donà	1545
Marcantonio Trevisan	1553
Francesco Venier	1554
Lorenzo Priuli	1556
Girolamo Priuli	1559
Pietro Loredan	1567
Alvise I Mocenigo	1570
Sebastiano Venier	1577
Nicolò da Ponte	1578
Pasquale Cicogna	1585
Marino Grimani	1595
Leonardo Donà	1606
Marcantonio Memmo	1612
Giovanni Bembo	1615
Nicolò Donà	1618
Antonio Priuli	1618
Francesco Contarini	1623
Giovanni Cornaro	1625
Nicolò Contarini	1630
Francesco Erizzo	1631
Francesco Molin	1646
Carlo Contarini	1655
Francesco Corner	1656
Bertuccio Valier	1656
Giovanni Pesaro	1658
Domenico Contarini	1659
Nicolò Sagredo	1675
Luigi Contarini	1676
Marcantonio Giustinian	1684
Francesco Morosini	1688
Silvestro Valier	1694
Alvise Mocenigo	1700
Giovanni II Corner	1709
Alvise III Mocenigo	1722
Carlo Ruzzini	1732
Alvise Pisani	1735
Pietro Grimani	1741
Francesco Loredan	1752
Marco Foscarini	1762
Alvise IV Mocenigo	1763
Paolo Renier	1779
Lodovico Manin	1789